# NO PRIZES FOR RUNNERS-UP

## The Nuts and Bolts of Election Campaigning

KOJO YANKAH
& DODZIE NUMEKEVOR

authorHOUSE®

AuthorHouse™ UK
1663 Liberty Drive
Bloomington, IN 47403 USA
www.authorhouse.co.uk
Phone: 0800.197.4150

Published by AuthorHouse  03/06/2019

ISBN: 978-1-5462-9785-7 (sc)
ISBN: 978-1-5462-9789-5 (e)

Print information available on the last page.

This book is printed on acid-free paper.

#  ACKNOWLEDGEMENTS

First and foremost, I would like to thank my wife Shemaat for standing beside me throughout my career and writing this book.

I would also like to express my gratitude to Roselyn for the support given to Dodzie, for without him this book would never have been written. These women have been the inspiration and motivation for continuing to improve and moving our careers forward. I also thank the wonderful children: Darryl, Chaela, Asher and Anelle for understanding on those weekend mornings writing this book instead of playing games. I hope that one day they can read this book and understand why so much time was spent in front of the computer.

I'd really like to thank Dodzie Numekevor for providing me with the opportunity to become the lead author for this book. I appreciate that he believed in me to provide the leadership and knowledge to make this book a reality.

I would like to express my gratitude to the many people who contributed in diverse ways to this book; to all those who provided support, talked things over, read, offered comments, allowed me to quote their remarks and assisted in the editing, proofreading and design.

Thanks to Sam Kwame Numekevor, Kingsley Karikari-Bondzie, Hayford Atta Krufi, Marlon Anipa and Charles Bissue for helping me in the process of shaping my political campaigning knowledge. Thanks to my May Arado, my publisher who encouraged me.

Last and not least: I beg forgiveness of all those who have been with me over the course of the years and whose names I have failed to mention."

## FOREWORD

Over the last decade, political campaigns have become sophisticated. The eagerness to identify and exploit the slightest competitive edge has gradually turned campaign strategy into a science.

Kojo Yankah, a policy analyst and campaign strategist and Dodzie Numekevor, a Communications practitioner, law graduate and a campaign strategist, having configured how data analysis and political theory are fusing and changing most ideas about political campaigns have come up with this book on campaign strategy; **No Prizes For Runners Up.**

The book takes a hard look at the use of data for modern political campaigning, and reflects on advances in Research, message development, communication strategy, funding etc. Simply, **"No Prizes For Runners Up"** is a manual about effective planning to win elections.

The book makes clear that a campaign should not simply be a calendar of events leading to an election but should rather define the goal and map out how to achieve that goal.

In my view, the principles in the book can be applied by all political parties and candidates, big or small, as they draw a picture of their electorate and ways to engage them effectively.

Finally, different political parties offer different analysis of the problems facing society and the solutions to these problems. These are the choices put before voters. But if those ideas are not communicated effectively to the voters, using appropriate language, through carefully selected mediums in which they can be heard and acted upon, chances are that, the political party or candidate will not be forming the government. Hence **No Prizes For Runners Up.**

*- His Excellency Papa Owusu-Ankomah*
*High Commissioner for Ghana to the United Kingdom and Ireland*

Luke 14:28–30 says, "Suppose one of you wants to build a tower. What is the first thing you will do? Will you sit down and figure out how much it will cost and if you have enough money to pay for it? If you don't, you might start building the tower but not be able to finish. Then everyone who sees what is happening will laugh at you. They will say, "You started building, but could not finish the job." Electioneering campaigns are no different—they need a plan to be successful.

## CAMPAIGN PLANS: ARE THEY REALLY THAT IMPORTANT?

Alice: "Would you tell me, please, which way I ought to go from here?"

"That depends a great deal on where you want to get to," said the Cat.

"I don't much care where," said Alice.

"Then it doesn't matter which way you go," said the Cat.

—Lewis Carroll, *Alice in Wonderland*

I lost you, right? We not talking about toddlers at Disneyland. Stay with me while we journey through the role of "Planning" in electioneering campaign.

Morale: If you don't have a coherent plan to execute the electioneering campaign, it's very likely the campaign will be making it up as it goes along, and there is a great possibility that defeat will be inevitable. Running a political campaign is one of the most challenging and exhausting but rewarding activities possible. On election day, either you win or you and your entire campaign team are fired (hence, *No Prizes for Runners-Up*). As you approach the final days of the campaign, this situation creates a huge amount of stress and pressure to succeed. While nothing can eliminate the stress of the countdown to election day, the proper organisation of a political campaign can avoid some unnecessary challenges.

This book is aimed at readers interested in knowing the full cycle of what needs to be done in order to win an election. The central role of this book is to address the role of planning in electioneering campaign. As you will come to realise when travelling the journey of this book, campaign plans aren't simply calendars of activities in an election campaign; campaign plans are much more than that. Good campaign plans should be written months and even years prior to elections so that the party-building and good governance work required to win an election or re-election are put in place with that clear strategic goal in mind. The written definition of that goal—and the map of how to get there—is the essence of any campaign plan.

Political campaigns can be an exciting experience, but if care is not taken, the euphoria can drown the goal. A great deal will happen between now and election day which will require some forethought and planning, you can then be prepared for all the twists and turns and, in many cases, control the situation.

While the given political landscape is an important factor in any campaign, in many cases the difference between winning and losing—is what goes on during the planning of the campaign.

## WHAT IS A POLITICAL CAMPAIGN?

A political campaign is a coherent series of activities that work to achieve the ultimate goal of winning the election. The set of steps outlined in this book will guide you through what these coherent series should entail.

It is argued that contemporary political rhetoric has moved from a focus on campaign message to a holistic view of the campaign process. This buttresses the fact that the campaign message alone will not deliver the expected results. On the contrary, it will take a comprehensive, well-thought-out plan.

## THREE TYPES OF POLITICAL CAMPAIGNS THAT MAY FALL SHY OF VICTORY DUE TO LACK OF PLANNING

The *first* type of campaign has not managed to develop a persuasive message to deliver to voters, and even more importantly, it does not have a target voter to persuade with the message. This type of campaign lacks direction from the beginning, and the situation will only get worse.

The *second* type of campaign that has managed to develop a concise, persuasive message and a clear idea of which voters it can persuade, but it lacks a reasonable written plan of what to do between now and election day to persuade these voters. This type of campaign will likely end up wasting time and resources as it wanders aimlessly toward election day. It is often distracted by the days' events, by things the opponent's campaign does, or by what is making rounds in the media, spending more time reacting to outside factors than promoting its own agenda.

The *third* type of campaign has a clear message, a clear idea of its voters, and a written plan in place to get to election day, but it fails to follow through on the plan, avoiding the hard work required day after day to get elected. This is a lazy campaign that makes excuses as to why it cannot do what it knows must be done and, in the end, makes excuses as to why it lost.

The *winning* political campaign is most often the one that takes the time to develop a persuasive message, target voters, and follow through on a reasonable plan to contact those voters directly till the last ballot is cast.

The goal of this book is to assist political parties and candidates in taking steps to running the winning type of campaign.

> *Note: The basics of any election campaign are deceptively simple. All campaigns must repeatedly communicate a persuasive message to its target voters. This is "the golden rule" of politics.*

A political campaign is, in effect, a communication process—find the right message, target that message to the right group of voters, and repeat that message again and again in accordance with your implementation strategy to secure victory. You don't have to invent the wheel. You just have to plan and execute. And that's what this book is about.

# CHAPTER 1

# RESEARCH, ASSUMPTIONS, AND ANALYSIS

> If you know the enemy and know yourself, you need not fear the result of a hundred battles. If you know yourself but not the enemy, for every victory gained you will also suffer a defeat. If you know neither the enemy nor yourself, you will succumb in every battle.

—Sun Tzu, *The Art of War*

The first step in every election is research. Your research should take into account the peculiar nature of the political terrain in which the campaign will be waged and the different sets of rules governing elections. At this stage of the process, you must use your time to find out as much as you can about the voters and your potential opponents.

Research and analysis are not frills; they are basic prerequisites for a successful campaign. For that reason, never neglect them. Budget for them from the beginning, and budget generously. After all, nothing is more costly than a lost election.

One needs to understand that every campaign is unique, even if some fundamentals can be applied to each campaign. To this end, you must have a complete understanding of the particular situation and the conditions in which your campaign will be waged. At some point in almost every campaign, someone will be tempted to say, "It is different here" or "You're not taking into account our particular situation." For example, how will voters react to the energy challenges of an industrial town, like Tema in Ghana, versus those of Cape Coast in the same country? Here is where you have the chance to demonstrate how different your situation really is.

*Why Research?*
- to help identify what you need to win
- to clarify campaign goals and challenges
- to know the voter
- to assess the candidate and the opponent

## HOW TO CONDUCT RESEARCH

When choosing research tools, one can distinguish roughly between qualitative and quantitative tools.

## QUANTITATIVE TOOLS—PAINTING BY NUMBERS

Quantitative tools enable you to describe reality with numbers. A classic example is "If the election were to be held tomorrow, who would you vote for?" The results can then be presented as percentages.

Quantitative analysis yields simple but robust statements about voter groups within brief periods of time. These include socio-demographic characteristics (including gender, age, income, occupation, religion, and origins), topics they care about, their assessments of certain politicians, and so on.

A group of persons representative of the general population can be surveyed in face-to-face interviews, on the telephone, or by the Internet. The number of people who need to be surveyed to yield representative results varies depending on what you are trying to find out and the overall population

A quantitative study can be helpful before and during the campaign. Before planning begins, the study offers a good basis for answering critical questions about the campaign's target group, allocating resources, and planning the budget. The insights you gain are a compass that can point you in the right direction throughout the campaign. Especially when you are unsure about whether you and your campaign are taking the right path and addressing the right people, a glance at the map of the electorate, the survey report, or the volume of tables can be very helpful.

During the campaign, such surveys can determine which candidates are popular, how the voters stand on a current issue, and who cuts the best figure during the campaign. Answers to such questions help not only the campaign. If skilfully disseminated, they can also influence reporting in the media.

## QUALITATIVE METHODS—GETTING CLOSER TO THE ELECTORATE

Qualitative methods, in contrast, depend on the observer's impressions. Generally, this involves longer, more detailed conversations and interviews or group discussions that offer the client an excellent overview of individual reactions to and assessments of a particular subject, message, claim, or poster. These qualitative research methods, while relatively subjective, yield astonishing information and insight.

However, qualitative tools cannot provide usable representative results or hard figures. They are nonetheless important campaign aids. The most widespread instrument is the so-called focus group, a moderated discussion among a small group that answers questions along predetermined guidelines. Socio-demographic criteria are used to cast the group. To the observer, these discussions are often a revelation since campaign organisers all too frequently forget to discuss their brilliant ideas with ordinary people. And by the time posters are hanging all over town, advertisements have been placed, and campaign spots have hit people's television screens, it is often too late. For that reason, focus groups—in closed, semi-anonymous spaces—save us from many mistakes or confirm our strategies. Some top candidates might find it useful to follow a discussion of their public appearances or see the puzzled faces when their names are mentioned. After all, self-perception is generally far removed from the way outsiders see us.

## KEY AREAS FOR RESEARCH

There are six key areas of research:

1. *The demography of the landscape.* Most African communities are made up of people from different ethnic, religious, and social backgrounds. Research on the demography of the area must be very thorough since it will subsequently help in formulating a campaign plan.

2. *Election rules.* The critical point to note at this stage is the type of election in which your party or candidate is running and the rules governing that election. In Kenya, for example, a candidate shall be elected president if he or she receives more than half of all votes cast in the election and at least 25 per cent of votes cast in each of more than half the counties. In Ghana, a person is deemed elected as a member of parliament if he or she receives a single vote more than each of the candidates in the race, or via what is commonly called "first past the post".

3. *The country/district or electoral area.* Once the rules are determined, you must gather information on the country or district in which the election is to be fought. You must aim to get as much information on the voters and the district as possible. Some of the questions that the research must aim to answer include the following: How large is the electoral area in which your candidate is running? What is the voter population of the area? How many polling stations will there be? Which parts of the area are more populated? And who are the main political

players? You will also need to ascertain the area's opinion leaders. For example, winning the support of chief fishermen, pastors, or Muslim clerics in an area can boost your chances and make your campaign run smoothly.

4. *The voters.* The voters in your electoral area need to be broken into manageable groups, for example, Kikuyus and Luo Kalenjin (Kenya); Yoruba, Ibos, and Hausas (Nigeria); Ashanti, Ewes, and Gas (Ghana). If research on voter demographics is detailed, it may later be used as the basis for developing a strategy for targeting, messaging, and contacting voters (this is discussed in detail in subsequent chapters). Some of the questions to be considered at this stage of game may include the following: What are the ethnic backgrounds of the voters? What are the ages of the voters within that ethnic group? Other issues to consider when conducting research on the voters include religion, gender, occupation/profession, place of work, and type of house they live in. Much of this information can be obtained from population census reports available from the relevant authorities, independent bodies, or the candidate's own teams.

5. *Past elections.* Who campaigned for the position on your party's ticket in past elections? How many votes did they obtain? Which parts of the electoral area did they hail from? How many people voted in past elections? What campaign messages featured prominently? Has the number of voters on the electoral roll increased or decreased? Has there been

an influx of voters of a particular background into the area since the last election? (For example, people from different ethnic backgrounds migrated to the western region of Ghana following the discovery of oil in commercial quantities.) What accounted for the migration? How did candidates with similar or different backgrounds and messages fare in past elections? These questions help measure the potential for growth since the last elections. Also, they may help you determine which strategies worked in past elections, what you can do differently the election you are about to contest, and which strategies and messages you need to maintain.

6. *Present elections.* The task at this stage is to look at the factors that may affect the election your candidate is about to take part in and the issues that concern the voters. The key here is to break down the issues that concern voters into local and national ones. Some of the issues may overlap, and it is important to take this into account. For example, an increase in the price of electricity may be a matter of national concern, but for farmers in a village in your electoral area, their concerns may be lack of water for their cattle. The mistake most candidates make is to assume national issues can be propagated in their local elections.

Other questions which research on the present elections should attempt to answer include the effect of the presence of certain candidates on your campaign. For example, what is the effect of the presence of an independent candidate who defected from your party? And what about candidates from the town or village your candidate hails from? Other matters your research must address in connection with the elections include:

a.  whether there are experienced party activists and election experts who can help your candidate (the advantage of getting these individuals on board is that they may bring their own supporters and followers, who may help boost your candidate's campaign)

b.  if it is a parliamentary election, whether it is politically smart to go all out for your presidential candidate (for the purposes of the 50 per cent +1 needed to win) or to run a parliamentary campaign

c.  research on the literacy/illiteracy level of the voters

d.  if you are the incumbent, which areas voters think you have performed well in and which areas you underperformed in

e.  which areas of the constituency are accessible by road, foot, water, etc.

f.  how many churches, mosques, etc., there are in your electoral region

## THE CANDIDATE

The candidate will be the most important person in your campaign and election efforts. Everything revolves around them. It is therefore essential that during your strategic planning sessions, you do an honest and candid assessment of their strengths and weaknesses.

It is important to look at the candidate from the point of view of the voters, your opponents, and key opinion leaders. One way of doing this effectively is to organise your assessment into different sections, such as the candidate's work in the community, their household or family (if the candidate comes from a family that is noted for charitable deeds and service to the community, they may benefit from this goodwill), their character and persona (most voters in Africa prefer and feel comfortable voting for politicians who are easily approachable and humble).

One of the challenges in this area is either reluctance on the part of the candidate's handlers to point out his weaknesses or failure on the part of the candidate to accept his weaknesses. In most cases, for example, past mistakes of the candidate were not brought out earlier in the strategic planning sessions because either the candidate was not truthful with his handlers or the campaign team thought the opponents would not find out.

In a nutshell, strategy is critical in campaigns; however, it must be built upon a solid knowledge of the conditions that predominate in a candidate's district. Attempting to marshal a complex campaign without a deep understanding of the prevailing social, economic, and political dynamics of a region is for many candidates a recipe for failure. Running a political campaign not grounded in empirical evidence can spell doom.

# CHAPTER 2

# GOAL SETTING

Too many candidates simply throw their hats in the ring, hoping they'll figure it out as they go along. Right? Wrong. Now that I've said this, one might easily conclude that I am not a dues-paying member of the "Let's See How It Goes" fan club. On the contrary, I am a firm believer of the school of thought that if you're running for office, you're running to win. If you're running to win, you had better know how to win.

Armed with your research information and your best judgement, you will now need to translate these research data into the number of votes you will need to win the election. This process is called the *setting the vote goal*.

## WHAT IS THE VOTE GOAL?

Simply put, your vote goal is the number of votes needed to win your election—and yes, you definitely need to know what this number is. Your campaign has one goal: to convince enough voters to show up to the polls on election day (or to vote early) and vote for you. The campaign should keep this goal in mind and make sure every decision that's made moves the campaign closer to this goal.

## SETTING A GOAL

What needs doing here is to determine what must be done to achieve that victory. Too often, campaigns forget to calculate how many votes will be needed to guarantee victory and determine where these votes will come from. They then spend their precious resources of time, money, and people trying to talk to the whole population instead of the much fewer voters they will actually need to win. Here you will reduce the number of voters with whom you need to communicate to a much more manageable size. If the research stage of the game has been completed as described earlier, by now, the campaign team should be able to determine the total population of your district, the total number of voters, the expected votes cast, the number of votes needed to win, and the number of households in which these voters live. Some of the answers that are needed here require you to look into the future and make some educated guesses, relying on your best judgement and the information you have found from past elections.

Let's take a look at some definitions pertaining to the vote goal. You must bear with me, as there will be a few numbers coming your way, but I will move heaven not to bore you.

*What is the total population of the district?* "Total population" is all the people who live in your district. This number will include children too young to vote and people not registered in the district. This number should be larger than the total number of voters.

*What is the total number of voters?* "Total number of voters" is all the voters in the district who are eligible to vote and can possibly vote in this election.

*What is the expected turnout?* "Expected turnout" is the number of voters who are likely to vote in that particular election. Not every registered voter will vote. Often, you can determine how many voters will vote by looking at past similar elections. If there was 70 per cent turnout in the last general election and there are no added factors to change the situation, you might figure that about 70 per cent would vote in the next general election, bearing in mind that the "plus or minus 5 per cent rule" is likely to apply in each case. In other words, if there are to be changes, you may want to estimate that a different percentage of voters will turn out the next round, possibly between 75 per cent and 80 per cent. In the case of Ghana, for example, changes are likely to take place. This is because during the period of four years which represents the voter cycle, the voter register will have been opened for voters who would have attained the voting age to register and subsequently exercise their franchise when the need arises.

*How many votes are needed to win?* This is a very speculative number. What you are looking for is the total number of votes needed to guarantee victory in your race. Again, in the case of Ghana, you need a simple majority of the votes to win if it's a parliamentary election and 50 per cent plus one vote when it comes to the presidential election—simply put, 50 per cent of turnout plus one vote. How many actual votes will guarantee your victory? You should be conservative and err on the side of too many votes rather than too few.

*How many households do these voters live in?* You can reduce this group yet again. On average, let us say that there are two voters per household. Some families may have three or four voters living in the same house. Some voters may be single and live alone. Now, if you think that a husband and wife are likely to vote the same way (although they don't always), you can sometimes assume that if you talk to one member of the family, then you can expect to get the second vote. So, how many households will you need to communicate with to receive the number of votes needed to win?

Let's consider the following scenario: Let say a typical constituency in the Central region of Ghana has a population of 70,000 people. Of this population, 20,000 residents are not voters, including children below voting age and other non-registered voters, leaving a total number of 50,000 voters. In the last general election in the constituency, there was 75 per cent turnout of voters, or 37,500 votes cast. This is how it plays out; assuming it will be the same next round and you are running for a presidential race, then your target is 50 per cent plus one vote, or 18,751 votes. If you figure an average of two voters per household, this would come to about 9,380 households. Let's round up the figure to 19,000 voters and 10,000 households. Now, you cannot assume that every voter you talk with will be persuaded to vote for you. So you should plan to communicate with a larger number of voters in order to receive the votes from 19,000 voters, or 10,000 households. Suppose you persuade seven out of every ten voters you communicate with to vote for you (however, in your campaign the proportion may be substantially less than that). In this scenario, you will need to talk to 54,000 voters, or 13,000 households, in order to be assured of support from 17,000 voters or 8,500 households (28,000 x 0.7 = 19,600 and 15,000 x 0.7 = 10,500). It is still a lot easier to talk with and try to persuade 15,000 families than it is to persuade 37,500. This whole process involves narrowing the group of people you need to persuade down to a much smaller size.

## GUIDE QUESTIONS IN DETERMINING VOTE GOAL

- How many people (not just voters) live in your district?
- How many of these people are able to vote in this election?
- What percentage of these voters do you expect to vote in this election?
- How many expected voters is this in real numbers?
- How many candidates will be running for this position?
- How many of these candidates could be considered serious?
- If the election were held today, what percentage of the vote do you think each candidate would receive?
- What percentage of the votes cast will be needed to win?

- How many votes cast in real numbers are needed to win?
- On average, how many voters live in one household?
- Do these voters living in the same household all tend to vote for the same candidate?
- If they do tend to vote for the same candidate, how many households will you need to receive the support of to guarantee victory?
- If you talk to ten average voters, how many can you persuade to vote for you?
- How many households will you need to communicate with for your message to reach enough voters to achieve victory?

Having determined the figures you need to secure victory, you will now need a plan to move this from the drawing board to reality. This leads us to the next chapter, which is "Campaign Planning".

# CHAPTER 3

# CAMPAIGN PLANNING

The will to win a political election campaign or the will to form a government is worthless if you do not have the will to prepare. Running into political election campaign without a strategy can cost you a fortune. It can also be stressful and truly disappointing after the race. However, how many candidates will go into an election with a winning strategy, and how many will not? How many political parties will go into election campaign with strategies to win more seats, secure enough numbers to form government, and how many will go into an election ill-prepared?

Political parties who wish to secure the numbers to become a major player in the formation of government and individual candidates who wish to run for public office must have in place an effective election campaign strategy.

One of my father's famous sayings as I grew up was "Plan the work, then work the plan." He said it so often that it got old, but it was good advice. His saying assumed that without a plan, there couldn't be any work, and without work, a plan was worthless. This diction, applied to political campaigns, couldn't be farther from the truth.

Planning a campaign is like building a house. First, you decide what to build and where; then you lay the foundations, upon which you create the visible structures and work on the details. The foundations of campaigning are clear objectives, and the blueprint is your campaign plan.

Campaigns are so hectic that it pays to take the time before they begin to research your strategy and develop a plan that you think will lead to victory. Truth be told, how long you've been in politics doesn't really matter. It doesn't really matter if you've worked on every campaign for the last forty-five years. The campaign needs a plan—a comprehensive, well-thought-out, written plan.

*Note: No campaign, regardless of size, should start without a campaign plan in place.*

## WHY A WRITTEN PLAN?

A written campaign plan provides a roadmap for your campaign. Without a written plan, the campaign will turn into a series of unplanned reactions to unanticipated events. The campaign plan should define the aims of the campaign and show how they can be achieved.

A campaign plan that has not been written down can make an already difficult task nearly impossible to implement. Whenever the campaign faces difficulties, it is important to have this strategic document on which people have agreed, and it must be there from start of the campaign. This plan may be developed in consultation with your advisors; "old hands", a campaign manager, or a consultant may take responsibility for writing the plan, in concert with other stakeholders. No matter who actually writes the plan, the candidate must be comfortable with the plan and support it.

While you should consult with all of the above people while writing a campaign plan, the only person you should give veto power to is the candidate. No other stakeholder should be able to hold up the plan. Gain everyone's input, make a decision about the strategy for the race, explain your decision to the stakeholders, allow comment, and then proceed. Don't let one chef spoil the soup that the entire team has worked on together.

Campaigns are tough and time-consuming. If you get into the heat of battle and the candidate spends all of his or her time re-thinking the plan, it can be a recipe for disaster. That's not to suggest that your plan won't change— it might—but you should change only the key strategies that you outline in your plan if something major happens. A well-planned and managed campaign can be flexible as the campaign grows or shrinks. Uncontrolled growth is nearly as harmful for the campaign as shrinking it. And you must make sure from the outset that the structure of the campaign can handle the growth. Otherwise, you will be tweaking the tactics (sometimes on a daily basis) but sticking to the major themes of your plan.

A strategic approach to campaigning has immense benefits. Thorough research and a well-designed campaign strategy and implementation plan can help you to:

- run for public office on a solid foundation
- be more confident and comfortable in your campaign

- use your limited time and resources strategically to maximise results
- know where you will concentrate your campaign efforts
- know what to do and what to avoid
- know where the race will go from the beginning
- know your position in the race well before the casting of votes and counting
- increase your chances of winning in the political election campaign and many more

*Note: Political campaigns are hectic. Your campaign plan provides a roadmap to success on election day.*

## DEVELOPING THE WINNING CAMPAIGN PLAN

Developing a comprehensive campaign plan requires that you complete some research to arm yourself with the requisite knowledge before completing the plan. You'll want to work in concert with your team to develop the best plan possible.

The most <u>important</u> phase in developing a successful campaign is to determine the reason for campaigning. Ironically, this phase <u>in particular</u> is often skipped. The objective has to be <u>specifically</u> decided and defined. It has to be written down, and everyone must understand it. For example, how many votes do we need to secure victory? Where can we <u>secure</u> these numbers? In the case of presidential elections in Ghana, this must be achieved during the first round or, a run-off will be imminent.

A surprisingly large number of campaigns fail because the objectives are vague. Establishing the <u>objective</u> is, without a doubt, the most <u>important</u> individual decision of the campaign. A small, well-built campaign with a clear <u>objective</u> is better than a large, uncertain one with vague <u>objectives</u>.

> *Note: An effective campaign requires strong team spirit and a shared objective.*

## COMPONENTS OF A SUCCESSFUL CAMPAIGN PLAN

Your campaign plan must be comprehensive. That is, it must address all the various activities your campaign will engage in—and in politics, many <u>activities</u> are vital to your ultimate win. A good campaign plan will include the following components, which will be addressed in detail subsequently:

*Targeting and demographics.* Who lives in your district? How do they break down across neighbourhoods, ethnicities, tribes, gender, occupation, age, religion, ideology, etc.? How many people will vote in this election? How many votes do you need to win? Which voters/areas are you targeting?

*Campaign message, issues development, and overall strategy.* What is your campaign's overall message/unified theme? What are your issues? What is the "question" of this election? What is your general strategy for success?

*Communications plan.* What paid media will you use (TV/radio/newspaper, etc.)? What collateral materials will be used (posters, T-shirts)? What is your plan for generating earned media (press coverage, etc.)?

*Grassroots plan.* How will you recruit and use volunteers? How will you run an effective get-out-the-vote operation? What will your strategy be for absentee ballots/election-day operations/door-to-door campaigning/etc.?

*Campaign budget.* How much do you need to spend, and on what, to win this election?

*Fundraising plan.* How will you raise the amount you need to spend to win this election? What events will you hold? Who will be on your Finance Committee? What major donors can you solicit? How will you raise money on the Internet?

*Campaign timeline.* What detailed steps do you need to take to implement your plan? By what date will you accomplish each one?

*Campaign staffing structure.* Who will be responsible for what in the implementation of this plan?

Each of these critical areas is important to your success and must be included in your campaign plan. Once your plan is completed, shop it around to the campaign's key stakeholders and get their input as well as the candidate's approval.

In the next chapters, we look closely at the various components that make up the campaign plan.

## MESSAGE DEVELOPMENT

As a candidate or political party, you are likely to face a challenge: how to craft a message that is meaningful, memorable, and persuasive and communicate that message with your targeted voters to get the votes needed to win the elections. Too often, campaigns start with the assumption that the candidate (or campaign manager, or media consultant) knows what the best message for the campaign is—without polling, without focus groups, without even running the idea past a few trusted advisers. No public campaign activity should take place without testing—and re-testing—the message involved. No campaign is strong without a good plan, and no plan is strong without a good message. Message is what drives the campaign plan; it sets the parameters in which the strategy is devised.

Let's settle a myth once and for all. Your message is *not* your strategy. These two items are often confused. *Message* is the answer to the question "Why am I running for office?" while *strategy* answers the question "How am I going to win?" In order to devise the strategy, the campaign must first plan its message. It must decide what it wants to say before it decides how it is going to say it.

The first principle in developing a persuasive campaign message is to relate it to an issue that the voters are emotionally concerned about. Drew Westen, in his book, *The Political Brain: The Role of Emotion in Deciding the Fate of the Nation*, asserts, "In politics when emotions and reason collide, emotion invariably wins." You may have a reasonable policy, but if that message does not connect with voters emotionally, you may not get the votes. For example, it is said that Jeb Bush had spent close to $50 million by the time he dropped out of the Republican Party primaries. Donald Trump spent much less and continued to win because he had a message that connected with the electorates. Always remember to make an emotional connection with the voters.

The message you send must be relevant to the voters because that message will either change or reinforce voters' perception.

## WHAT IS A "CAMPAIGN MESSAGE"?

Simply put, your message is the overriding theme of your campaign. It's the big-picture answer to that big-picture question: Why are you running for this office? It's the theme that separates you from your opponents. It's the broad statement of the values that define your candidacy, the values from which every single issue you talk about gets its force and substance.

Your campaign message is one of the keys to winning your election. Campaigns are, by their very nature, communications exercises. Much as an advertising campaign for a traditional product seeks to sell the product, the job of a campaign is to "sell" a candidate, period. The way you do this is to define and advertise what in the business world would be called a "brand" but in politics is called "your message". For example, recent and well-known campaign messages include:

- Change: Barack Obama
- Better Ghana: John Atta Mills
- Positive Change: John A Kuffour

## DEVELOPING THE "MESSAGE"

One of the tasks that every campaign must undertake from the start is determining which issues to concentrate on and which messages surrounding these issues work best. By taking polls, focus groups, etc., your campaign can determine the mood of the electorate. Using this data and comparing it against your candidate's views, the campaign can decide which issues and messages to emphasise and which to downplay.

Of course, simply testing your message is not enough. You need to get feedback from those you test with, be it by phone survey or in person. Review your assumptions. Take to heart the comments and guidance you receive, and, if it is viable, make the necessary changes to ensure that your message will have the desired impact.

## DEMOGRAPHICALLY SPEAKING

The first step in crafting the campaign message is to find out the demographics of the district the candidate is running in. This can usually be done by reviewing census data, voting records, and other public documents. The demographic survey can discover who the voters are. During this step, the campaign should learn everything it can about the makeup of the district, including age, gender, race, occupation, party registration, voter turnout, and any other statistic which will be useful for the campaign. These components, as mentioned earlier in the book, should be taken care of at the research stage.

## DIVIDE AND CONQUER

The next step for the campaign is to break the voters in the district down into useful categories. This categorisation should start with large groupings. For example, as in the case of Ghana, the constituency may have a makeup of 46 per cent NDC, 48 per cent NPP, and 6 per cent independent. Drill down through increasingly more defined categories (e.g., 15 per cent of NDC women are between the ages of nineteen and twenty-five).

The campaign should use the benchmark poll to attach issues to these groups. For instance, the poll may have shown that the large majority of these NDC women between nineteen and twenty-five are most concerned with jobs creation. Armed with the demographic data showing who the voters are and what they care about, the campaign can begin to draw a clear picture of the district.

## BUILD YOUR COALITION

After categorising the voters, the campaign should look at its own strengths and weaknesses to decide what coalition of voters it needs to utilise to win the campaign. The campaign should be able to figure out approximately how many votes it needs to win, and this should be taken into consideration in crafting the message.

> *Note: The campaign message must succinctly but compellingly answer the question "Why should the voters vote for me?" This message should be narrow enough that it is clear, yet broad enough that several issues can be drawn from it and used throughout the course of the campaign.*

## YOUR MESSAGE SHOULD TIE INTO CORE HUMAN VALUES

While not everyone cares about the exact same issues, a number of values are important to almost everyone. These values are:

- *Safety.* How safe is the country under your watch?
- *Health.* How will the temperature of the health of the nation fare under your governance?
- *Financial health and well-being.* Can I provide for my family? How is my job? How secure is my retirement? Will my kids have a better financial life than I did? Do I own my own home?
- *Morality.* Is our country headed down a morally defensible path?
- *Children's future.* How secure is the future of kids if you get the nod?

*Note: People will vote for a candidate who shares their values, who cares about the same things they care about, and who can demonstrate that he or she is "qualified" to make a difference.*

The candidate or party must have a set of values to accompany his message because voters care about the people they cast their votes for. This means the candidate should be able to tell voters about things he did in the past or is presently doing that make him a credible candidate for the position. The issue to consider here is to build trust. For example, a candidate may succeed in espousing the concerns and aspirations of the voters in his or her campaign message, but if voters do not trust him to make good on his promises, he may not get the votes. This means that the character of the candidate needs to be worked on.

## USE YOUR "MESSAGE"

The only way to get the voters to know your message—to associate the values of your message with your candidate—is to incorporate your message into everything you do.

Every aspect of your campaign, from fundraising to door-to-door campaigning to your volunteer program, must revolve around your message. Every communication you send out must relate back to your message. Every event, every activity, every project your campaign undertakes must relate to your message, spread your message, and incorporate your message. Your goal, at the end of the campaign, is to make sure that every voter walks into that voting booth thinking about your campaign message.

Say, for example, you're running for president in a keenly contested presidential election in Ghana against an incumbent. During their tenure, businesses are folding, taxes have gone up, and their cronies have gotten rich. Your campaign team has decided that the cutting issue of this campaign is incompetence and corruption. You campaign message? "Better Ghana. We Deserve It."

Maintaining your message as the focus of the campaign won't be easy. Your supporters, your opponents, and the media will all be encouraging you to go "off message" to address their pet concerns. Don't do it! Stick to the script you developed, and when election day comes, those voters are going to be so upset about the president and his corrupt cronies that they'll go into the polling place saying, "Better Ghana? We *do* deserve it!"

If you are the incumbent, on the other hand, your message should include your achievements, and you should remind voters about this. This also means you should be in a position to admit your failures and ask for time to fix them because voters prefer honest candidates to dishonest ones.

Everything your campaign does must relate back to your message, or it will never stick in voters' minds. When you hold a press conference, it ties back to your message by noting all the fraudulent contracts given to friends of the government. You hold "Take Back Our Government!" rallies, and dub your demonstrations, "Government for All". Each and every tactic and move the campaign makes must revolve around your message. This means it is perfectly fine to have a layered message, but it should feed into the overarching theme. For example, while voters in a typical fishing community in Ghana may be concerned about premixed fuel for their outboard motors and pair trawling by bigger foreign vessels, voters in more plush residential areas may be concerned with the activities of armed robbers. The campaign message must therefore be tailored to speak to the aspirations of the various areas.

## FACTORS TO CONSIDER WHEN DEVELOPING THE "CAMPAIGN MESSAGE"

Your message must:
- differentiate your candidate or party from your opponents
- be simple and clear
- be short and precise, easy to repeat
- make implications about the record and character of your opponent
- be about the future because people are interested in hearing what the future holds for them and their families

## COMMUNICATION STRATEGY

Everything you have done up to this point—all the research, goal setting, audience targeting, and message development—has brought you to this point. Now you need to decide which technique is the most efficient to communicate with this large group of people and convince them to vote for you. There is no point in having a great message if the voters do not know about it. Avoid the mistake of making your communications decisions based on fleeting sentiments.

Now that you have a clear, concise, and effective message, use that message to persuade your target group of voters that your candidate is the best choice. Voters need to know what your message is, and they need to hear it many times before it registers. You must repeatedly communicate a persuasive message to people who will vote. The campaign has to get the candidate's name and message in front of the voters continuously. Any communication that doesn't move the candidate closer to victory is a waste of valuable resources.

When planning your campaign's communication strategy, you must remember that you have finite resources. Every decision to do something is a decision not to do something else. For example, when you spend money on television, you do not have that money to spend on posters. Time spent greeting shoppers at the market is time taken away from going door to door. It is important to budget all three resources—time, money, and people—so that you have them when you need them and so that all three resources are used most efficiently. You want to make the largest impact on the voters while using as few of these resources as possible.

For example, let's say your campaign is ready to put up posters. At this point, many campaigns will simply send out volunteers to find houses and walls to paste them on; however, smart campaigns will start out by asking questions: Where are the people who would most likely vote for the candidate if they only knew about him? What high-visibility areas do our targeted voters pass through regularly?

> *Note: Modern political campaigns shouldn't waste valuable time or resources by trying to communicate with everyone who lives in the region/district. Many people won't be registered to vote or won't be likely to vote on election day (according to their past voting behaviour). The number of voters you communicate with will ultimately be determined by what you can afford.*

## TYPES OF VOTER CONTACT

*Door-to-door.* One of the most effective ways to persuade voters is to go from house to house, door to door, talking to individual voters one at a time. You are able to hear their problems and tailor your message to meet their individual concerns and gauge their level of support. Obviously, this is going to be very time-consuming.

*Phoning.* The telephone can be used to persuade voters to vote for your candidate, identify supporters, and remind those supporters to go vote for your candidate. Each of these should be a separate phone call. Most often, the phone is used to identify supporters and turn out the vote. Both of these can be relatively short calls. Phone calls can be made either from volunteers' homes or from a central location with many phones. These central locations, called phone banks, can be either businesses or organisations with a lot of separate phone lines already in place that allow the campaign to use them after office hours to call voters. They can also be extra phone lines put into the headquarters for just this purpose. Either way, phone banks have a number of advantages over having volunteers make the calls from their homes. First, the campaign can supervise the phone calls at a phone bank and make sure that the calls are being made and effectively delivering the agreed message. Second, the volunteers gain support from other volunteers making the calls. It is often important to share the experience, either good or bad, of the last phone call. Finally, the campaign has immediate control over the process, can deal with problems immediately, answer questions, and receive instant feedback. Sometimes the script the volunteers are using when they talk to voters does not work and must be changed. Or sometimes the campaign may want to shift from phoning one constituency to another quickly. This can be more easily done at a phone bank. When both using a phone bank and having volunteers call from home, it is important to have clear written instructions for the volunteers, including the purpose of making the calls and an easy-to-follow script of what to say on the phone when talking to voters. It may also be important to explain what not to do, such as argue with voters. Volunteers should understand that it is important to make as many calls as possible, as quickly as possible, and that arguing with voters will only slow them down, will be unlikely to change their minds, or, worse, will make them even more determined to go and vote for your opponent.

*Literature drop.* This is where volunteers go door to door, leaving a piece of literature about the candidate at each household. A large number of volunteers can cover a large area relatively quickly, and because you know that the houses are in the constituency, you know that only potential voters are being reached. The volunteers are not talking with voters, so they do not identify supporters, but they can leave a reminder to vote at the supporters' homes just before election day.

*Literature handouts.* Your campaign can also hand out literature wherever people gather in large numbers. This could be at markets, factory gates, public transport stations, etc. While this may be a lot easier or quicker than the literature drop at the voters' homes, it is less targeted because you are not certain that the people who take your literature live in the district or can vote for your candidate. Often this type of activity is targeted at a particular issue that will concern those gathered in that area.

*Visibility.* Anything the campaign does to catch the voters' eye. This can be billboards by the side of the road, posters at supporters' houses, posters on poles, stickers on cars, volunteers or the candidate waving to traffic, the candidate's/party's name on T-shirts, pens, etc. While this may raise the voter awareness about the campaign and the name recognition of the candidate, it can only reinforce the campaign message, but it can be a very poor method of persuading voters. However, in some remote constituencies, if the poster is accepted by a voter, it could be an indication that they will vote for you.

*Endorsements.* The candidate can meet with various opinion leaders in an attempt to persuade them to support the campaign. These opinion leaders can be alternative media editorial boards or representatives of issue-oriented or community-based organisations. The effectiveness at reaching voters depends on the influence these leaders, or their organisations, have on the voters. Time should often be spent winning this support early in the campaign, when voters aren't paying attention to the election but the opinion leaders are. The campaign can then communicate these "third-party endorsements" in their campaign literature or news releases to show voters which local leadership support your candidate; knowing that others in the community support your candidate gives permission for other persuadable voters to do the same.

*Paid media: television, radio, and newspaper adverts.* Unfortunately, you will not be able to count on journalists to provide you with all the publicity you will need for your campaign. You may need to purchase additional publicity in the form of newspaper, radio, or television advertisements. This is a less targeted way to reach voters than canvassing the constituency. While you reach a broad audience, again, it is not clear that everyone who hears or sees your advertisement is able to vote for you or is in your target audience. It is particularly good at reinforcing a message that is already being delivered in person, such as by door-to-door visits.

*Internet web pages.* The most recent addition to the list of voter contact methods is placing a web page on the Internet. It should be remembered that the Internet is a passive form of communication, meaning that it does not go to the voters; the voters have to come to it. So, while you may be able to get some press from introducing your website, and while it can be an inexpensive way to convey a lot of information to those who are interested, it is not effective at reaching a particular, targeted audience.

*Combining various methods.* Different campaigns at different levels will use different combinations of voter contact to reach voters. With the varying resources of time, money, and people, the combination of voter-contact methods is unlimited, and no two campaigns will ever be alike. This is why it is critical to collect all the data possible on the district, the voters, and all the candidates. Then the campaign must develop a workable written plan to deliver the message.

Remember, no matter what type of campaign communication you are sending out, it must stay on message. Your campaign message is the driving force of your campaign communications. If you're talking about issues, how do they support your message? If you're doing a negative advertisement, how does it show that your opponent will not be able to fix the problems and deal with the issues you lay out in support of your message? Remember, message is king.

With all these things in mind, ask the following questions as you consider the various types of voters contact:

1. How much does it cost in time, money, and people?
2. Do you know which voters are being reached?
3. Are the voters being persuaded?
4. Can you find out if the voters support your candidate and will actually go out to vote for your candidate?

## FIGURING OUT YOUR CATEGORY MIX

People are often persuaded when they hear the same thing from many different sources. If they hear that you are a good candidate from a respected civic organisation, if they meet the candidate going door to door, and if they see some persuasive campaign literature, then they will more likely remember the candidate and vote for him or her. None of these contacts should be left to chance. A well-organised campaign will make sure that all these contacts happen and that the same message is delivered each time so that the message reinforces itself each time.

One of the key decisions that your campaign will need to make is what mix of the above communications categories you will focus on and when. For example, when should your ads be comparison pieces? When should your ads be about issues?

## A GENERAL GUIDE

A typical scenario might look like this:

- Ms Abban gets an oversized "bio" postcard at her door.
- Two weeks later, Ms Abban notices your campaign billboard on her way to work.
- The next week, Ms Abban sees your posters and signs start sprouting up all over the neighbourhood.
- Two weeks later, Ms Abban gets a knock on her door to say hello.
- One week later, Ms Abban gets a comparison piece from your campaign dropped at her house.
- The next week, Ms Abban starts to see/hear your TV/radio ads.
- The next few weeks, Ms Abban is invited to attend a campaign event/rally.
- The cycle above can be repeated as often as possible.

- Three weeks into voting, Ms Abban gets a reminder to go vote and a get-out-and-vote call/text from one of your campaign volunteers.

Getting the candidates name and message in front of the voters early and often—and doing so through a variety of media and tactics—substantially increases the odds that Ms Abban knows who you are and what you stand for.

As the campaign communicates with voters, try to judge their level of support. As you identify voters, you will want to have some method of keeping track of them and their levels of support. You can use a simple card file or, even better, a computer database that you can continuously update, sorting the data to meet your needs. This database must be as accurate as possible. Do not consider someone a supporter unless they have told you so directly. Often people will not want to offend you or argue with you if they have not made up their mind or actually support your opponent.

## CAMPAIGN BUDGETING: HOW MUCH SHOULD YOU SPEND AND HOW?

Planning a campaign budget takes cold calculation to avoid winding up short of money during the closing (and most critical) days of the campaign.

Budgeting is a crucial element to winning the race. Writing an accurate budget is imperative for success. This cannot be overemphasised. Most campaigns running neck and neck with their opponent fail to cross the finish line first because of financial constraints late in the campaign; this can be the result of poor planning and poor budget strategy. In practical language, budgeting has to do with how to plan your expenses, where to trim back, and when to go on a spending spree.

Just about everything you do in the campaign will cost something. You should estimate how much each of the tasks you hope to accomplish will cost and develop an overall budget for the entire campaign. Your campaign budget should not be a wish list but a realistic list of what will be needed to implement your campaign plan. Written budgets are the only tools for tracking expenditures, providing goals for fundraisers and keeping the candidate and campaign from spending without thinking.

Review your timeline and calendar to determine at what point in the campaign you will need the money. By organising your budget month by month or even week by week, you will be able to anticipate what amounts you will need and at what time. You will thus avoid the age-old problem of cash-flow difficulties, and your fundraisers will understand what money is needed and when.

Having high-, medium-, and low-budget plans is useful in case your fundraising does not go as well as anticipated. You can better plan and save money for spending priorities like voter contact activities.

> *Note: Campaigns everywhere need to spend the bulk of their funds on voter-contact activities.*

## A GUIDE TO ALLOCATING FUNDS IN YOUR CAMPAIGN BUDGET

Administrative costs, including office machines, office staff, and phones, should be less than 20 per cent of your budget. Voter-contact costs, including television, printed materials, and door-to-door workers, should consume 70 per cent to 80 per cent of your financial resources. Research, including polling, should take up less than 10 per cent of your budget.

*Developing a budget.* The keys to successful budgeting are setting the right goals, careful monitoring, paying the right prices, and knowing a few tricks of the trade.

What should your budget actually look like? For starters, you should include spending categories on the vertical axis and months on the horizontal axis. As you get closer to election day, you will want to do a weekly, and then a daily, budget. Your spending should be divided into two main categories—persuasion and non-persuasion. In the persuasion section, you should include such voter contact expenses as TV, mail, phones, press research, field, and polling. Your non-persuasion section should be subdivided into administrative overhead and fundraising. As a general rule, the campaign should spend 70 to 80 per cent of its funds on persuasion.

> *Note: the percentage of your budget spent on overhead will be greatly determined by the length of the campaign.*

Some budget guidelines:

- Voter communication: 70–80 per cent
- Field: 5–15 per cent
- Fundraising: 5–10 per cent
- Administration: 5–10 per cent
- Research and polling: 5–10 per cent
- Earned media: 1–3 per cent

Realistically, the campaign should be able to decide how much money can be available to place in coffers right away and how much you can be committed to it later on. Seed money is important. If potential donors see that you believe in yourself, they too will believe in you. For the remainder of the money, set realistic fundraising goals. If you are challenging an incumbent, no matter how unpopular he or she might be (or how unpopular you think she or he is), do not expect to raise significant money. Once you have figured out your fundraising goal, commit to a feasible plan to raise this money. Remember, if you calculate your personal commitments and fundraising goals too low, you will run out of money. The key is to be realistic; I cannot stress this enough. Remember, there are few "sugar daddies" in politics and no free rides.

How do you spend what you haven't got? You guessed right. Am talking about revenue.

## SOURCES OF REVENUE

*Personal money.* The first resource the campaign will be your own money. People will often gauge your level of commitment based on how financially committed you are to the project. It's said "Show me where your treasure is and I will show you where your heart is."

*Specific interest groups/PACs.* If you are a lawyer, for instance, the need to tap into your local or regional association and affiliated specialities for money and endorsements cannot be overemphasised.

*Major donors.* Research on regular donors to political campaigns. Giving is a behaviour, and those who have given will give again.

*Events.* Events can be a very expensive way to raise money but are utilised routinely. Events take time to set up and usually require some kind of invitation as well as catering costs. Oftentimes, however, events, particularly with special guests, are the only way to interests potential donors.

*Loans, personal and other.* If you are willing to put your name on a loan and don't mind paying it back, win or lose, this can be another source of money.

*In-kind exchanges.* Many goods and services are available in-kind, meaning people who can't or don't want to give money can provide printing services, catering services, etc.

## EXPENDITURES

Once you have determined how much money you can reasonably expect to raise, the next step is to assess how much you will need to spend.

*Political environment/history.* Primaries generally have fewer voters you will need to contact. Look at the history of similar races and how many people have voted in recent elections.

*Who's in the race and how many?* Is it a primary with two or eight people that will determine your strategy and budget, or is it a presidential with four contestants?

*Are you a known quantity?* If you are already well known, you have an advantage because name identification is critical in helping drive your message. Candidates not as well known will have to spend more money.

*How will you contact voters?* Voters need to hear your message over and over to understand it.

*Party expenditures.* Will others be spending money on your behalf that will benefit your campaign?

> *Note: Budgeting for campaigns can be a difficult but very important task. Plan ahead and make sure you do not go broke as election day approaches. Be realistic and do not cut corners on the essentials. If need be, find expert hands in drawing up a budget if you want the campaign to be competitive and professional, focused on delivering victory. The difference between a win and a loss may be a better finance strategy.*

## WHY A FUNDRAISING PLAN?

Campaigns are hard, and they move fast. In the heat of battle, it can be hard to know what to do next or where to focus your campaign's limited resources.

The candidate and the campaign team (we assume) sat down and mapped out what they need to do to win. Now, they must sit down and in the same vein develop a plan to raise the money to do those activities which will ensure the successful implementation of the campaign plan.

That's where a fundraising plan comes in. You should write your fundraising plan before you even launch your campaign because once the campaign actually begins, there will be so many different things to do and so many fires to put out that it can be impossible to sit down and write a well-thought-out fundraising plan. During that period, before the campaign starts, your candidate and team will have clear heads and time to think about the best strategy for raising the money you need to win.

While the fundraising plan will vary based on the campaign strategy, certain variables are fundamental to every plan.

## THE FINANCE COMMITTEE

The term *Finance Committee* can be deceiving. This committee isn't really responsible for executing the fundraising plan—that task falls on the shoulders of the campaign manager, campaign staff, and volunteers working with the fundraising director. The role of the Finance Committee to provide a starting point for the campaign's political fundraising network.

All members of the Finance Committee should be supporters of the candidate who have a wide range of contacts they can solicit to support the campaign. Each member is generally expected to contribute to the campaign and then pledge to locate a certain number of others to do the same. The committee can be composed of local businessmen, professionals, and political contacts, among others.

## WHOM TO ASK

Consider asking the following people for their support:

1. *Friends and family.* More likely than not, your friends and family are the ones who best understand your vision and support your objectives. While you probably will not depend on them for the majority of your financial backing, your friends and family

are a great resource to build your bank account and, by extension, your credibility. Because it takes money to make money, this group operates as an effective springboard to sell yourself to the next group you want to target.

2. *Issues people.* There are many types of issues people—labour unions, business groups, religious groups, women's groups, ethnic groups, environmental coalitions, etc. Start with the groups most aligned with your message, and sell to them that their concern is your concern. Then move to the groups partially aligned with your message; remember, no group of people is completely homogenous, and politics often makes strange bedfellows. Examine your campaign's issues. There just might be people you have not considered as potential supporters who share your concern on that one topic. And do not forget one of the most important groups of people to target—the people who hate your opponent. Whether they support your message or not, they very well might support you financially only because you are not him (or her).

3. *Influence buyers.* These are people who like to win. Investing money into a campaign is just that—an investment. People don't want to bet on the wrong horse. This is especially true of the big donors. They will wait and see if you have established yourself, your campaign, and your assets. If it appears you are a credible candidate, one with a chance of forwarding their objectives, they will put their money on you. Again, you must establish yourself

first by building your money with the first two groups so that when you decide to sell your message to the deep pockets and other influence buyers, you represent a winning commodity.

## WHO SHOULD DO THE ASKING

1. *You!* The candidate is the best person to do the asking. Have face-to-face "sit downs" with people. Your supporters will find this personal engagement extremely compelling. And you must ask them for a specific amount. Tell them specifically what you need—general support is not productive. Phone calls are also effective. Donors are impressed with the candidate who takes the time to personally pick up the phone and ask for their support.

2. *Friends asking friends.* Have your people talk to their people. Friends asking friends to give you financial support extends that intimacy which is so effective in fundraising. Again, this networking will allow your treasury and credibility to grow exponentially as people see that you are someone with wide appeal, and more importantly, a winner worth betting on.

## HOW TO ASK

1. *Mass customisation and personalisation.* You, the candidate, cannot devote all your time to fundraising, although sometimes it may seem as if you are. Granted, you should spend at least four

hours a day (and often more than that) raising funds, but this is still a small percentage of your time. Instead, pretend to do number one and number two of "Who Should Be Asking?" by using mass customisation and personalisation.

2. *Online fundraising.* As technology evolves, one cannot rule out the effectiveness of emails. Now, with email, you can send out a mass, customised, and personalised email a month out, two weeks out, even days out from the election. Second, imagine the rush that the donor receiving the email will feel when he can immediately help your campaign by making a credit card contribution right then and there. Today, not accepting online donations is virtually political suicide—the only thing you are losing is the ability to raise more money. And there is no reason not to. To this end, why not set up a website that can accept credit/debit card donations?

3. *Target, target, target.* The key to raising money is targeting your donors. Do not send mailings to environmental groups detailing your stand on health issues, and do not ask those who can pay big to pay little or vice versa. This type of missed targeting is a waste of time and money. It is not only ineffective in maximising the fundraising potential of your donors, but it may be counterproductive as well, alienating your supporters by demonstrating you are not personally attuned to their concerns. Therefore, you must dedicate resources to the strategies listed above—targeting, customisation, personalisation, and online fundraising.

> *Note: Be prepared to devote resources to fundraising. This means time (especially the candidate's time) and money (hiring staff and investing in good technology to assist you). Like most things, the right resources can make all the difference.*

## TIMELINE

Similarly, the fundraising plan needs to answer the question "When do we need the money?" Generally, political vendors require partial, if not full, payment up front. They do this because of the volatile nature of political campaigns. Thus, in order to send out a mail piece or perform a GOTV effort, the campaign needs to have the funds up front.

> *Note: Just because you have a written plan doesn't mean it can't or won't change during the course of the campaign. You shouldn't change your fundraising plan willy-nilly, but if circumstances change for your election campaign, you may need to revise parts of the plan. That's OK, but be sure to make those changes in writing and to make sure that your entire team knows that the plan has changed. You want to make sure everyone on your team is working on the same page.*

## THE MOST IMPORTANT PARTS OF YOUR POLITICAL FUNDRAISING PLAN

*Deadlines* and *responsibilities* are the two most important parts of any political fundraising plan. For every single strategy you have in your fundraising plan, you should have a list of action steps that will be required to make that strategy work. And for each action step, you should list the person who will be responsible for carrying out the action and a deadline for completion.

For example:
Fundraising event, 15/06/2016
Put together host committee, 01/02, Stephen
Secure venue, 12/02, Charles
Send out invitations, 20/02, Kwame
Make follow up calls, 27/02, Stephen, Kwame, and Committee
Finalize menu, decorations, and event flow, 15/04, Rita
Final follow-up calls, 30/4, Stephen, Kwame, and Committee

## THE COMPONENTS OF A SUCCESSFUL POLITICAL FUNDRAISING PLAN

*Fundraising target.* You should begin by setting your goal, which should spell out how much needs to be raised for the project. This should be defined in specific monthly targets that should fit into the campaign spending strategy.

*Assumptions.* This includes assumptions you are making in formulating the plan. Every campaign makes assumptions as it plans its fundraising. Some examples of possible assumptions may include:

- assuming that your candidate will be the "establishment candidate" and receive funding from your political base

- assuming that certain major fundraisers will line up to support your candidate
- assuming that the party will raise so much from its membership

List your assumptions up front and know that if one of the assumptions doesn't bear out, you may need to rewrite part of the plan to map out a strategy for dealing with the new reality.

*Resources.* Do you currently have in place any resources to get you started? What infrastructure/resources do you envisage needing to see the project through? Your resources include, but are not limited to, fundraising staff, a donor database, marketing materials, websites, and mobile money.

*Fundraising tactics.* Each fundraising tactic should list action steps and responsibilities. This is the section where you lay out, in as much detail as possible, all the different ways you are going to raise money for your campaign. Each tactic should get its own subsection with action steps, deadlines, and responsible persons. Common tactics include: events, online fundraising, Finance Committee, major donors, personal solicitation by the candidate, affinity groups, and fundraising networks.

> *Note: It's imperative to create a strategy for staying in touch with your donors and prospects.*

## ACTION STEP TIMELINE

I cannot overemphasise the importance of setting action steps in each of the sections of the plan, which lists what needs to be done by which deadline in order for the plan to succeed.

This will not only help measure progress but allow anyone who reads the plan to get a good picture of all of the activity that is currently going on, see what the deadlines and goals are, and know who is responsible for each.

*Now, do it!* With a detailed fundraising plan in place, the campaign is ready to execute the fundraising strategy. By following the plan and continuously tracking fundraising efforts, fundraising won't be as taxing on the campaign or the candidate. That way, the campaign can raise the money it needs with as little hassle as possible.

*Grassroots strategy.* Although there are many school of thoughts when it comes defining "grassroots strategy", it generally includes all the activities that keep the candidate, volunteers, and members of the campaign team in direct contact with the voter. Simply put, the person-to-person or one-on-one campaign. Grassroots activity is the single most effective way to reach swing voters. Posters works well, broadcast media works OK, but grassroots campaigning really connects with voters.

> *Note: It takes time and people, long hours, and lots of organisation, but grassroots campaigning works.*

## WHY IS GRASSROOTS CAMPAIGNING SO EFFECTIVE?

Grassroots campaigning yields results because all people, including voters, like to build relationships. They like to hear from real people. They like to talk, go to events, ask questions, and entertained. People don't like to feel sold, they like to feel like they are hashing issues out in their mind and making their own decisions.

> *Note: In order to execute a robust grassroots organisation, an efficient volunteer pool, trained to knock on doors and get the people out to cast their ballot on election day, is a must.*

Components of a successful grassroots organisation:

- volunteer strategy
- door-to-door strategy
- get-out-to-vote strategy (GOTV)

*Volunteer strategy.* A lot of planning is needed for your volunteer operation, and it must be taken seriously. Disorganized volunteer operations can be a huge headache for campaigns—often, it's better not to utilise volunteers than to run a shoddy volunteer program. No matter the type or ability of your volunteers, they all need training and support from your campaign. Even if the volunteer in question is already well versed in how to do the job you are assigning them, they will need to spend some time learning the ropes of the specific campaign in question, getting to know the campaign's message and issues, educating themselves about the candidate, etc.

*Door-to-door strategy.* Knocking on voters' doors is the only opportunity the candidate gets to meet voters face to face. When done effectively, not only can one gauge their popularity and acceptability, but one has the opportunity to address voters' concerns and correct propaganda that is negatively affecting voters' perception. It also helps to build name recognition for the candidate. Door-to-door campaigning also helps to builds credibility because it shows that the campaign is a living, breathing thing and that it has a sound support base.

What makes a successful door-to-door campaign?

- *Preparation*. The doors that you will be knocking must be targeted. The team to do the knocking should know their brief with the necessary resources readily available.
- *Knowing the times to knock*. What time is the best to knock so as not to inconvenient voters?
- *The follow-up*. During your visits, accurate notes should be taken so informed decisions can be made regarding revisits. This is where classifying voters into what I call the "traffic light system" is crucial. Also, be sure to send voters any additional information they have requested.

*Get-out-the-vote strategy (GOTV)*. Why have a well-organised and well-run campaign if you will not have a strategy to get the votes in the box? Even worse are campaigns that are made to believe that they have immense support from the public and that voters will, of their volition, queue for hours to cast their votes. You couldn't be more wrong. The simple truth is you need a well-detailed plan on how will you execute your election-day strategy. This is where your GOTV strategy becomes essential.

> *Note: An organised GOTV and monitoring operation is critical on election day if you will be declared the winner.*

How does one justify having spent valuable weeks persuading your target audience that you are the best candidate only to have them fail to go to the polls on election day and vote for you? Individual voters often feel that their single vote does not matter. They need to know that they are part of something bigger and that their support for your candidate is important. Often a simple reminder—either a phone call or, in the case of the elderly, arranging for transport to ferry them to polling station—can be enough to ensure that they vote. The "get out the vote" (GOTV) effort is often viewed as a separate phase of the campaign. In fact, it should be viewed as the final phase toward which everything else in the campaign builds. If you compare a political campaign to a business selling a product, in this case selling the candidate to the voters, then the eve of election day is the only day in which you can make the sale. It is important that the voters be motivated enough to "buy your product" on that one day. The deadline for all the campaigning and particularly the GOTV part of the campaign is the eve of the election-day polls. Either you are prepared to make that final push or you are not. There are no second chances.

## WHAT IS GOTV

GOTV is all activities designed to turn voters out on election day. The campaign teams answer to getting supporters to go out and vote on election day. This effort can be accomplished in many different ways, but the various methods differ in one important factor, whether or not the campaign knows who is being contacted. In areas where a candidate has considerable support—say, seven out of every ten voters will vote for them—it is not necessary to identify supporters. You will know that the more voters you remind about election day and make sure that they vote, the more votes your candidate will receive. In these areas, you can organise what is called a "blind pull" of voters, or pulling everyone to the polls regardless of whether you know whom they are supporting. In areas where the support is very strong, the campaign can put up signs reminding voters about election day and encouraging them to vote. They may want to phone as many of the voters as possible to make sure they turn out or send in a car with a loudspeaker telling people it's election day it's and time to go vote. In other areas where support is less certain, you will want to remind only those voters you know support you. It is therefore important to have spent time identifying which voters will support you well in advance of the GOTV effort. Once you have developed a database or list of supporters, it is important to have the resources and the means of communicating with them in the short period of time just before the election. It is therefore important to budget enough time, money, and people and to have a realistic plan of how you will get in touch with your supporters.

## GOALS

Your GOTV team should target at least something in the region of 10–15 per cent of the supporters you need to win to cast their ballot. To this end, the teams focus will be on identifying your supporters and getting as many of them as possible to go vote. Their role should be clearly defined as they are not responsible for persuading people to support your candidate—that is the job of the rest of your campaign structure. Theirs is to identify voters who already support the candidate, based on feedback from the campaign team, and then motivate them to go and vote.

> *Note: Get-out-the-vote campaigns take lots of time and effort, but they are worth it. Your campaign's plan to turn out its supporters can be the difference between victory and defeat.*

## CONCLUSION

Your grassroots organisation will play a key role in your victory on election day, but only if you stick with it. It may seem slow going at first, recruiting and training volunteers, holding rallies where ten people show up, going door to door where no one has ever heard of you, but stay with it. Your efforts will build upon themselves, and before you know it, your grassroots campaign will be the liveliest (and most fun) part of your effort.

## TIMELINE

Campaigns require advanced planning, action taken on multiple fronts, and the smooth operation of numerous activities, often simultaneously. It can be difficult to keep track of how and when to implement all the components of a successful campaign. What are the detailed steps you need to take to implement your plan? By what date will you accomplish each? Here you will be addressing the issue of your timeline.

Each of the activities that will be embarked on in your quest to securing victory should be executed within a certain timeframe. Having a timeline in place helps the team measure performance to success rate. After a campaign plan has been agreed on, a timeline and a calendar listing the key tasks that must be accomplished and the dates they must be accomplished by should be clearly drawn. This among other things will help the team to ascertain if the campaign is on track or amendments are necessary. For example, if the launch of the campaign is fixed for a certain date and this does not materialise, then one can measure how the campaign is faring.

This timeline in most cases will primarily be informed by various dates that will be important to your campaign. For example, election day is one obvious important date. Other important dates may be filing deadlines, exhibition of voter register, and dates when you are required by law to make certain reports. All these dates should be kept on a master campaign calendar. Early in the campaign this may be a monthly calendar, but as election day draws closer, you may want to develop a weekly or even daily calendar that provides more details. Subsequent dates with timelines will then be added to this calendar. For example, important events or meetings that the candidate must attend should be diarised.

The campaign must have a system for dealing with invitations. This system should include ways to decide if an event is important enough to attend and ways to decline invitations that the campaign decides are not important.

In addition, all various voter contact activities should be included in the calendar. Here it is important to distinguish between activities that will require the candidate and those that may be handled by the campaign and volunteers. Because certain voter contact activities will happen over a long period of time and overlap with other activities, it is also necessary to develop a timeline of events that will provide more details about time, money, and people involved in each activity.

It is important that the candidate does not keep their own calendar because this often leads to confusion about who needs to be where and when. Develop a master calendar for the campaign that will include all the important dates and all the important activities of the campaign.

To complete the process, you will need to be vigilant at counting, making sure all Ts are crossed and Is dotted. This is the most critical of all. You cannot afford to fail at this process, as all your efforts will have been in vain.

## CAMPAIGN STRUCTURE

Campaigns cannot revolve around a single person. It's about teamwork. Getting the right team from the word go is one of the most crucial strategic decisions you will have to take. Its worthy of note that members of team may not necessarily be from within the political party in question; rather, they must be capable of delivering on the task. While all campaigns are different and thus have different needs when it comes to campaign organization, there are certain vital positions that almost every campaign must fill. Whether the position is filled by paid professionals or volunteers, these positions and their roles must be clearly defined to ensure the smooth running of the campaign.

## THE CAMPAIGN TEAM: WHICH PEOPLE, WHAT FUNCTIONS?

Political campaigns, like anything else, benefit from experience. The more times an individual has been involved in past political campaigns, the better prepared they should be for the next political campaign. Having the advice or assistance of someone who has experienced the various phases of a campaign can be very helpful to the candidate and the campaign.

Arguably, a small campaign team should be encouraged. That notwithstanding, this is not always possible because of the political need to include certain functions and factions of the party. The general rule is a team of five people and never exceeding fifteen, subject to the size and dynamics of the campaign. Positions that must be filled from the outset include campaign manager, finance chairman, fundraising director, communications director, and volunteer coordinator.

> *Note: The guiding principle is to have a team that can be trusted and able to convene and react to issues in good time. A campaign team full of technocrats with no experience, no matter how talented or quick-witted, will rarely deliver.*

## THE ROLE OF THE CAMPAIGN MANAGER

It is the campaign manager's task to make sure that all planned issues are carried out on time and as well organised as possible. In effect, the role of the campaign manager is to run the campaign. This must be someone in whom the candidate has complete confidence. After all, this should be the most important thing in both of their lives for the relatively short period of time that the campaign will last. In a sense, the candidate is the heart of the campaign, and the campaign manager is the brain.

> *Note: The candidate should not fall for the temptation of wanting to run their own campaign. They either do not choose a campaign manager or choose someone they think they can manipulate. In either case, they end up spending too much time making decisions that should be left to their manager, which takes time from their main job, which is meeting voters and donors.*

A campaign manager must make sure the candidate is scheduled to meet voters. They must deal with, or otherwise supervise those who will deal with, the press/media, the finances, the other methods of voter contact, and everything else planned and unplanned during the campaign.

## VOLUNTEER COORDINATOR

Volunteer groups can be necessary evils during campaigns. As the case may be, there will always be people who will want to help in their own way towards delivering the victory of the campaign. Some of these individuals may metamorphose into groups, which, if care is not taken and managed, can veer into waters that may be detrimental to the efforts of the campaign. To address this issue, it's always advisable to have in place a coordinator to oversee and manage their activities.

## FUNDRAISING DIRECTOR

Refer to the "Fundraising Plan" chapter. The fundraising director should be responsible for coming up with ideas on how to generate funding to finance the campaign. In effect, he or she is responsible for the day-to-day management of fundraising activities.

## FINANCE CHAIRMAN

Their role often seems to conflict with that of the fundraising director, but they are meant to perform different roles. Refer to the "Fundraising Plan" chapter.

## SAMPLE CAMPAIGN PLAN

Campaign plans are great tools. No campaign, no matter how small, should be without one. They provide guidance, timelines, and budgets and should generally be followed in the successful pursuit of elected office.

It's important to remember, though, that execution is the real key. No amount of planning can make up for the fact that a candidate doesn't go door to door or the Finance Committee isn't raising enough money. The only way to win a campaign is to get out there and do it. Using this plan, your campaign will be off to the right start.

Equally important is the knowledge that politics is fluid by nature and that all campaigns and campaign plans must be flexible. While "sticking to the plan" is generally great political advice, there will come times when something extraordinary happens in a campaign that necessitates a change. Don't get stuck doing something that doesn't work just because it is in the plan. Figure out what needs to be changed, change it, and move on.

Lastly, measure your progress. Use polls, research, press stories, campaign finance reports, and/or word of mouth to make sure that the plan is working. If not, use your best judgement in re-configuring your campaign plan.

## POLITICAL ENVIRONMENT, ASSUMPTIONS, AND ANALYSIS

Joe Bloggs is running on the ticket of NPP for the Cape Coast Constituency. The general election will be held on Tuesday, 8 November 2016. Our assumed general election opponent is Martin Smith, the incumbent. We are not currently aware of any independent candidate.

## DISTRICT/CONSTITUENCY ANALYSIS (JUST AN ANOLOGY)

Cape Coast South has a total population of just fewer than 3.5 million residents. The median household yearly income is approximately 5,000 Cedis. The median age is 36.8 years. Of residents who report a religious affiliation, the largest religious affiliations in Pentecostals (49 per cent), followed by Catholics (19 per cent) and Moslems (2 per cent). There are approximately 1.5 million voters registered. Voters do not register by party.

## POLITICAL ENVIRONMENT

This election is being held in a time of great political change, and thus the political environment is volatile. We believe that this election will see "average turnout". National issues which are likely to affect this election include the downturn in the economy and the power crisis. The local issues that are most likely to be felt in this election include job losses, schools, and education.

## CANDIDATE PROFILES

Joe Blogg is a professional businessman, married with three children. His wife, Rhonda, is a homemaker. This is Joe's first run for office.

## CANDIDATE STRENGTHS/WEAKNESSES ANALYSIS FOR JOE BLOGGS

*Strengths*
- has control of own schedule, can dedicate significant time to run for office
- charismatic speaker with good command of the issues
- appealing background story

*Weaknesses*
- presumably low name ID
- will need to raise a significant amount of money for a challenger campaign
- political inexperience
- NPP Party is weak in Cape Coast South

## CANDIDATE STRENGTHS/WEAKNESSES ANALYSIS FOR MARTIN SMITH

*Strengths*
- incumbent
- high name ID
- proven fundraising ability
- NDC Party is strong in the constituency

*Weaknesses*
- perception as an ineffective follower
- unclear messages in previous elections
- corruption and uncaring

## MEDIA OUTLETS

The campaign needs to compile a comprehensive media contact list for this election cycle. This media contact list should include name, outlet, address, phone, and e-mail information for all television, radio, newspaper, and blog/web journalists that the campaign will be communicating with over the next two years.

## RESEARCH/POLLING

The campaign and candidate have a good command of the issues and a core team of volunteers ready and willing to perform research functions. The campaign also understands the importance of professional political polling in determining where to focus valuable resources and in what manner. To those ends, the campaign should place an early focus on the following:

*Opposition research.* The campaign research team should compile a research dossier on Martin Smith, including involvement in corrupt deals, news clippings, and speech excerpts. The candidate and campaign should compile this opposition research now for use throughout the campaign.

*Issues research.* The campaign research team has already begun researching key issues that may come up in this election. The research team should continue this work by putting together comprehensive research dossiers on each of the key issues, including statistical data, news clippings, and policy reports from think tanks across the political spectrum.

*Polling.* There are several important types of polls in political campaigns:

- The *benchmark poll* or *baseline poll* is taken at the beginning of a campaign, before the campaign really begins its activities. This type of poll measures the starting point of the campaign—where the voters stand before they hear the issues the campaigns raise, what the name recognition of a candidate is before he begins to campaign, and what the different demographics are, such as age, ethnicity, and occupation.

- A *tracking poll* is taken several times over the course of the campaign to monitor the campaign's progress. Progress is generally measured in terms of how well the campaign is doing compared to its performance on the baseline poll. Most campaigns take several tracking polls throughout a campaign, and in large races, it is not uncommon for a campaign to take a tracking poll every day during the last two or three weeks of the campaign.

- *Issue* or *message polls* are taken to craft and hone the campaign's response to certain issues or to clarify and enhance the campaign message by testing different themes with the voting public.

- A *focus group* isn't really a poll, per se. Basically, in a focus group, a number of people are brought in to speak with a moderator all at the same time, and the moderator leads a discussion to determine the group's views on the questions he is asked. Focus groups are generally videotaped so that they can be examined after the event. Focus groups serve a different purpose than polls. Instead of trying to get accurate results that reflect the views of the public, as polls do, focus groups attempt to see the real, live dynamic that presenting the campaign's message to the group creates, what objections and concerns they have, etc.

The campaign does not have the financial resources at this point to conduct a baseline poll or to test messages through polling.

## GENERAL ANALYSIS OF CAMPAIGN ENVIRONMENT

1. Joe Bloggs has never run for office before; thus, he still has relatively low name ID. Raising this ID will be required in order to win.
2. Fundraising is key. Cape Coast South is a big constituency, and it will take vast resources for the campaign to succeed.
3. The opponent has name recognition and will have the money needed to run a competitive campaign.

4. The current political environment is unpredictable.

*Immediate action steps:*
- Perform opposition research.
- Begin issues binders with key issues research and media clips.
- Compile comprehensive media contact list.

## PRECINCT TARGETING

This is a unique and difficult election in which to perform precinct targeting, for two reasons:
1. *Lack of voter registration by party.* Because voters do not register by party, it is difficult to determine core voters.
2. *Changing vote patterns.* Recent election returns have shown that after several decades of declining vote numbers, the NPP is moving back towards competitiveness.

While it is normally preferable to have several election years represented in targeting data, we actually believe that in this circumstance, with rapidly changing conditions, 2012 provides a good view of the mood of the electorate. The analysis will capture a race where the NPP won, a race where the NPP almost won, and a race where the NPP lost by a wide margin.

The complete targeting data, including past voter history, is presented in a spreadsheet that is included with this plan. The important conclusions from this data are presented in the following table:

## TARGETING ANALYSIS/WHAT ALL THIS MEANS

This is an unusual election. Because of the demographics of the constituency, in order to win, our campaign must receive a significant number of votes from voters who lean towards the NDC. This isn't a "base" election; this is an election where we will have to reach across party lines and win NDC votes.

The good news is, it can, and has, been done before. These wins should be instructive to our campaign. In order to win this election, the campaign must:

1. *Focus on the swing districts.* In our targeting analysis, the swing districts are those districts where the margin of victory is small, no matter which party wins. NPP PCs who win do well in these districts, and those who lose do poorly in these swing districts. The campaign should dedicate a significant amount of time and resources to winning the swing districts.

2. *Hold on to the base.* In addition to winning the swing districts, the campaign must hold on to the lean and base districts, these areas, which normally vote NPP by a significant margin, must vote heavily. In order to do so, they will need to know his name and his message.

3. *Reach into NDC lean districts.* Finally, in order to win, our campaign should go on the offensive, spending some amount of time and money in NDC lean districts—those districts that usually go NDC by a moderate margin—in order to limit losses in these districts and garner additional votes.

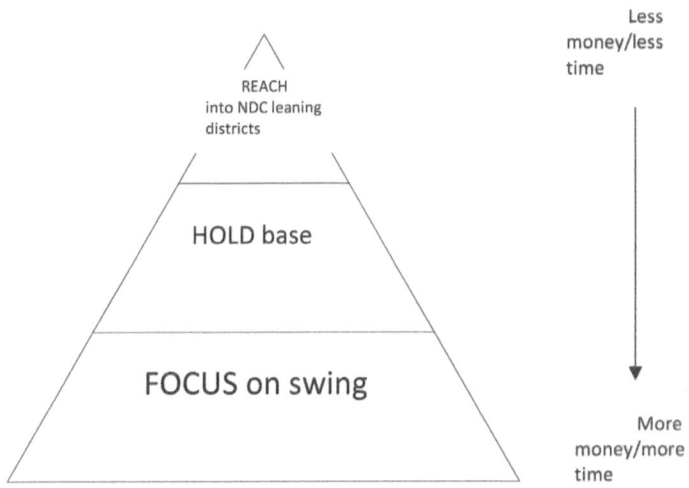

Thus, our precinct targeting will use the district lists as analysed above and will be based on the following strategy for the general election:

- less money/less time
- more money/more time

The one area the campaign should not focus on is opponents' base districts. It is unlikely the campaign will have the time and/or money to effectively outreach here, and these areas take the most time and money to make the smallest impact.

We will need NDC to win. The place to reach out to those NDC, for this campaign and in this election year, is first in swing districts and then in NDC lean districts. The only reason the campaign should focus on NDC base districts is if the campaign has an abundance of money and staff/volunteer time and other resources.

## VOTE TARGET

Based on the historical voting data, the campaign should expect a general election turnout of approximately 895k voters. Thus, to win, Joe must receive 550k votes. Everything the campaign does must be geared toward that number.

## INDIVIDUAL VOTER TARGETING

In addition to targeting the districts noted above, the campaign should use care in all of its communication methods to engage in individual targeting, targeting only those individuals who can (and are likely to) vote and to be open to your message. This targeting is done at the individual voter level and requires the campaign to acquire up-to-date voter lists from the EC.

How does individual voter targeting work? First, the campaign should never waste money by using resources to contact non-voters, unless the campaign has enough money and staff to run voter registration drives (more about those later). Thus, if you're sending direct mail, only send it to registered voters. If you're going door to door, only knock on registered voters' homes.

Similarly, you can cut down on your expenditures by targeting not only those who are registered to vote but those who are likely to vote.

*Immediate action steps:*
- Acquire constituency map that shows legislative districts.
- Acquire an up-to-date voter list from the EC.

## CAMPAIGN INFRASTRUCTURE AND STAFFING

Campaigns are serious endeavours and should be approached professionally. Run your campaign like a business—plan your work, execute your plan, and hold people accountable for their assignments. To operate effectively, the Joe Bloggs campaign needs the following campaign infrastructure:

*Campaign office.* The campaign will need to lease headquarters space to centralise campaign operations and provide space for meetings, staff, and volunteers.

*Regional campaign offices.* The campaign should be ready to open two to four regional campaign offices.

*Campaign database system.* The campaign should acquire a fundraising and volunteer management database system to use for this election cycle. This database system should easily printout campaign finance reports, track donations and pledges, and maintain donor/volunteer contact information. Several off-the-shelf packages should meet these needs.

*Consultants.* The campaign will benefit from working with professional political consultants throughout this process. The campaign will most likely need the following:

- a general strategy consultant—immediately
- a media consultant/ad production team/ad buyer (one company)—next year
- a pollster—as soon as possible
- a web design consultant—as soon as possible

*Volunteers.* The campaign has already started attracting volunteers. These volunteers, and hundreds more like them, will be a key to our success. The campaign should have a procedure in place for tracking volunteers, thanking them, and constantly updating the list of activities we need volunteers to complete on our behalf.

*Staff.* Currently, the campaign is operating with only one full-time unpaid staff member. This must change. The campaign is in desperate need of a professional staff to handle campaign tasks, and all full-time personnel need to be paid for their efforts. The suggested campaign staffing structure for the Joe campaign is shown below. All hires are subject to change (needed sooner, needed later, not needed, unable to afford), based on campaign needs, political environment, and fundraising success.

While the strategy of the campaign may dictate changes to this list, generally, the senior staff should be brought on board utilising the following order of hiring priority:

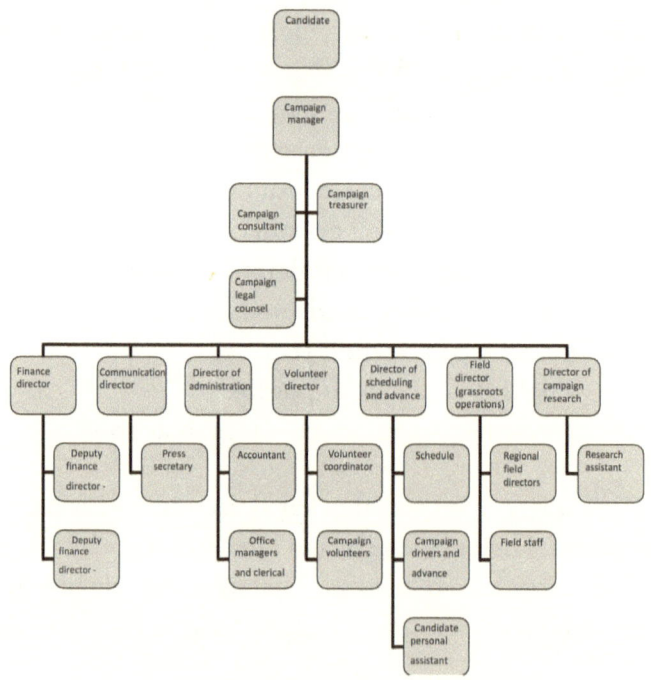

1. Candidate
2. Campaign manager
3. Campaign treasurer and legal counsel
4. Campaign consultants (general consultant)
5. Finance director
6. Communications director
7. Volunteer director
8. Director of scheduling and advance
9. Field director
10. Director of campaign research
11. Director of administration

Junior staff may then be brought on as needed depending on which areas of the campaign are seeing the most growth momentum.

## STAFF POSITION DESCRIPTIONS AND SUGGESTED SALARY RANGES

*Campaign manager*: CEO of campaign, director of all campaign activities ($17,000–$20,000 per month).

*Finance director*: Develops campaign fundraising strategy and directs all campaign fundraising activities and tactics ($10,000—$12,000 per month).

## CAMPAIGN MESSAGE AND STRATEGY

In order to break through the clutter of the campaign news cycle and motivate our unique-blend NPP, swing, and NDC-leaning voters, the "Joe for Parliament" campaign will need to broadcast a strong and compelling message to the electorate. The message is one of the most important facets of a campaign. People vote for someone who they think cares about the same things they care about and who they believe is uniquely qualified to make a difference. The message must speak to concerns the voters already have, and they must be emotional, not frivolous concerns. Perhaps the most important thing to remember about our message is it must be unified. That is, our campaign can only have one message. The message must be well crafted and must pervade everything we do. Every issue we speak on, every positive thing we say, every negative thing we say about our opponents must relate back to our campaign message.

Our message must also be positive. People want a positive can-do attitude from their political candidates. We will compare and contrast and will place them in a negative light, but our main campaign message must be a positive one.

## THE ISSUES THAT MATTER IN THIS ELECTION

Incumbency has its advantages, including a willing press, access to funds, and the ability to move legislation to influence the election. Running against an incumbent has its advantages too, as every incumbent invariably makes people mad, builds a track record we can run against, and provides a high-profile "villain" for our "good-guy" message.

This is certainly true with Smith. In informal conversations, it has become clear to the campaign that the top negative issues identified are:

1. lack of management ability and failure to lead
2. corruption

In addition, we must be cognizant of our unique electorate. Our campaign must develop a message that not only plays off of Joe's strengths and Smith's weaknesses but also one that appeals to moderates and swing voters.

## THE QUESTION OF THE ELECTION

The question that we want voters asking when they go into the polling place is, "Who is going to actually do something in Cape Coast South (CCS) to clean up the mess our country is in?"

We'd like the voters to use the following logic:

- Our country faces a lot of problems.
- Everyone in CCS just talks and talks—nothing gets done!
- Martin Smith has been there too long—and has gotten nothing done.
- Joe Bloggs believes in CCS.
- He's the son of a single mother; he grew up poor and pulled himself up.
- He's a doer, not a talker, and he believes CCS's best days are ahead.
- He'll help clean up this mess.

## THE MESSAGE

The theme of our message is clear: Reform, open and effective. Our campaign must present that message in a clear, succinct, positive light. The campaign message statement should be

"Joe Bloggs: Leadership with you in mind". This message must pervade everything the campaign does—all communications that the campaign puts out, all speeches, all contacts, the website, everything. It hits our key points: honesty and openness, a leadership that works, change and reform.

## THE ISSUES

Now that we have our message, we must identify several issues that will highlight that message, as well as the difference between our candidate and our opponents. Several of the issues should be "positive" issues that deal only with our candidate, while several should be "negative" that deal with our opponent. During the initial phases of the campaign, we will focus almost exclusively on raising Joe's name ID and using our positive issues. During the general, we will switch to using both the positive and negative issues.

Suggested positive issues:

- *Fiscal responsibility.* With the economy in decline, he's got a plan for cutting out the waste.
- *Real leadership.* Joe will pledge to hold at least one open town hall meeting each quarter. He will welcome the comments and suggestions of everyone.
- *Revitalizing the local economy.* Utilizing his position at Parliament, Joe will work with government and local leaders to bring businesses and jobs to CCS

Suggested negative issues:
- *Ineffectiveness.* Martin Smith doesn't have a plan other than her own re-election. The economy crumbled

around her, and she just followed the NDC leadership. Where is her plan? Where is her backbone?

- *Where in the world is Martin Smith?* This speaks to lack of accessibility.
- *Additional issues.* These will be raised through opposition research.

## GENERAL CAMPAIGN STRATEGY

The strategy for this campaign is as follows:

1. Raise Joe's name ID in NPP-base, NDC-lean, and swing districts.
2. Sway independents and moderates to vote for Joe through our message of effective, independent leadership.
3. Identify which independents are planning to vote for Joe.
4. Move registered NPP and those independents that we have identified as supporters to the polls on election day.

This strategy will be implemented using the grassroots and communications strategies that are outlined later in this plan.

## COMMUNICATIONS PLAN

The communications and grassroots plans contain the lynchpins of our strategy. These two plans contain the tactics that will allow us to get our message out, identify our supporters, and get out the vote.

## THE BASICS

Remember that everything that we do in our campaign—particularly as part of our communications plan—must point back to the message we devised above. Before beginning serious communications efforts, the campaign must develop several basic pieces of the communications apparatus:

1.  *Website.* The campaign already has a website up and running, and it provides a good foundation for our efforts. The campaign should now take a close look at the website, revamp it, and edit it for our campaign roll-out. Some of these revisions should include: (1) editing for grammar and spelling; (2) adding the campaign logo and colour scheme; (3) adding photos; (4) making it easier to navigate and to donate.

2.  *Photos.* Suggested photos include: (1) the candidate; (2) the candidate in front of a desk; (3) the candidate at a local landmark; (4) the candidate at a meeting, talking with others; (5) the candidate having a "candid" discussion with one other person, perhaps a senior citizen.

3.  *Stump speech.* The candidate should refine his stump speech to come up with a pithy, message-driven speech of five to ten minutes for use at forums, community association meetings, etc.

## THE "QUESTION" OF THE ELECTION (REPRISED)

Voters generally decide an election by formulating a question, which they then answer with one of the candidates. For example, in the 2000 presidential election, the question was "Who is most likely to bring change to Ghana?" The answer was "John Kuffour."

As mentioned above, the question we want to pose to the voters is "Who is going to actually do something to clean up the mess our country is in?" If that is the question, we win because the answer is "Joe Bloggs."

We must jump out ahead of our opponents and work in a diligent and methodical way to make sure that our question is the question of the election.

## THE GOALS

Our communications operation has two primary phases:

During phase I, our communications goal will be simple: to raise Joe's name ID in a positive manner, with an emphasis on our message. The message is important. We must not only get Joe's name out before the voters but must also tie him to the message of effective and active leadership for a better tomorrow.

During phase II, our communications goals will be: (1) to continue to raise Joe's name ID, and (2) to sway independents to vote for Joe by contrasting Joe with our opponent and by raising our opponent's negatives.

## EARNED MEDIA

Earned media will be a key component of getting our campaign message out cheaply to the electorate. "Earned media" consists of all free media hits on television, radio, and the Internet.

The campaign should plan to generate earned media by:

1. staying in direct, regular contact with journalists
2. providing prompt and courteous replies to media inquiries
3. generating real news and following up with the media to ensure that the news is covered in each media outlet

As much as we want to believe that the media will just cover Joe's campaign because he's a great candidate, the truth is that generating earned media takes work. The key is to remain in constant contact with the press but not to be overbearing.

In the initial stages of the campaign, the campaign manager should be responsible for dealing with the media, answering questions, and scheduling interviews with the candidate. Once a communications director comes on board, he or she will take over these responsibilities. The candidate should *not* be in direct contact with the media unless the campaign manager or communications director sets up an in-person or phone interview for the candidate. Many campaigns have seen disastrous consequences when a communications director is holding off a member of the media (for good reason) and the candidate does an end run and answers a series of questions on the phone or via e-mail.

The media needs one contact; make it the campaign manager or communications director.

As noted earlier in this plan, the campaign must develop an accurate and comprehensive media list to guide our efforts.

Additional "media advisories" may be used to direct the media's attention to various events that the campaign may hold around the state.

It's important that the same day press releases are sent out, someone from the campaign calls each media contact to make sure they got the release and see if they have any questions. This is key, as reporters are generally very busy and don't open e-mails often, at least until they are called and alerted to the contents of the release. When these calls are made, the person making them should be prepared to discuss the release with the reporter.

Also, remember that the media only wants to cover real news, not fluff. The trick for the campaign is generating real news while staying true to our message. The media wants to cover news, but we want them to cover our message and reinforce our message in the minds of the voters.

Examples of "real news" that the media might want to cover, and that also easily ties back to our message, could include: the campaign kickoff, the opening of a campaign office or website, "Joe's walks across market", getting a key endorsement, etc. In addition to these regular press releases, the campaign should target a smaller group of reporters with story pitches, suggestions, and exclusives.

## MEDIA KIT

Immediately after compiling the media list, the campaign should develop a media kit containing Joe's bio, our walk piece or other brochure when available, a campaign factsheet, a good photo of Joe, and a short profile of our message and key issues. This press kit should be personally handed out by Joe when he does in-person interviews and can be mailed to the most important reporters (the ones we want to develop close relationships with). The media kit *must* be professional and attractive looking.

*Paid media.* The campaign should utilise paid media to effectively get its message out throughout the state.

*Billboards.* Most political consultants are not big fans of billboards, and generally I agree that money is better spent elsewhere in a campaign. In this campaign, though, I think they could be an effective part of our paid media mix. One of Joe's biggest problems is the need to raise his name ID. Assuming that billboards can be acquired for a reasonable price, the campaign should introduce a professionally-produced billboard campaign aimed at raising Joe's name ID and targeted at the large metropolitan areas and the medium-sized population centres.

*Television.* Television advertising will form the largest portion of our overall campaign budget. The campaign must have a professional television advertising message that brings Joe's message directly to the voters. The campaign should engage a media production firm/media consultant to develop our television advertising and plan media buys.

*Paid media, timing.* As a rule, paid media is used during the middle and end of a campaign. People have short attention spans, and campaigns have limited resources; thus, our campaign's use of paid media shall be as follows:

## MATERIALS

The campaign should design and use the following other campaign materials:

1. *Candidate walk piece.* Mentioned above, the campaign needs a brochure or oversized postcard-type piece with the logo, great photos of Joe, his bio, and some information on the campaign message and issues, as well as a way for the reader to sign up to help the campaign (such as directing him or her to the website). This piece will be used not only for going door to door but as the campaign's "standard" piece, handed out at events, rallies, and fundraisers; given to the press; and generally used in all campaign activities.

2. *Buttons/stickers.* We recommend using circular lapel stickers. They look like buttons but don't damage clothes and cost less.

*Immediate action steps:*

- Edit and update website.
- Write and edit stump speech.
- Get photos.
- Compile media kit.

## GRASSROOTS PLAN

The grassroots operation includes all the "on-the-ground" tactics the campaign will use during the election.

## PURPOSES OF OUR GRASSROOTS ACTIVITIES

The purposes of the grassroots activities are the same as the purposes of the rest of the campaign: to build name ID and sway independent voters. The grassroots plan, however, has one additional key goal: to identify voters who support Joe and to move them to the polls on election day. Accomplishing this task will require good information, a strong plan, and lots of help.

## BUILDING OUR SUPPORTER FILE

Because the grassroots operation will come into contact with voters on a daily basis, it is imperative that everyone involved in grassroots activities is prepared to collect voters' names and contact information and that the campaign has a system in place for storing these names and using this information.

The goal, of course, is to build a list of supporters who we can move to the polls on election day—voters who say they plan to vote for Joe. We need to get these people to the polls! The best way to do that is to stay in touch with them. Start building a supporter file on day one—and then stay in contact with them. Our goal is to make them feel as if they are part of our "team".

## FINDING AND USING VOLUNTEERS

The campaign should make every effort to find and recruit volunteers to help with its efforts. Volunteers should be asked to do one (or more) of several activities:

1. Hold a meet and greet event with Joe at their homes, for five to ten people.
2. Go door to door or pass out literature for the campaign.
3. Put up a yard sign.
4. Recruit additional volunteers.
5. Help fundraise.
6. Work the polls on election day.

*Note: The best way for us to find volunteers is to ask.*

Of course, volunteers will not be able to help us unless we are clear as to what we need them to do. Each super-volunteer should get a "job title", a clear definition of their responsibilities, and a packet of information to help them complete their jobs. If we have enough volunteers, some could be made into "area captains" for different neighbourhoods.

## CAMPAIGN GRASSROOTS ORGANIZATION

The best way to get our message out through grassroots channels and keep a steady flow of support coming back to the campaign is to develop a strong Joe grassroots organisation. This takes time.

We should constantly be on the lookout for people on the ground who support Joe and who could take on a volunteer leadership role with the campaign. The campaign should develop a corps of "team captains" who lead our grassroots efforts. These team captains should be appointed for as many areas as possible.

Team captains should be presented with campaign materials and a list of responsibilities, as well as a list of rewards. Samples of these include:

*Joe Blogg's Team Captain Responsibilities*
- Find five volunteers to form your town team.
- Hold one meet and greet event with the candidate each quarter.
- Have your team go door to door.

*Team Captain Benefits*
- They receive a "Joe's Team Captain" embroidered polo shirt.
- They receive priority invitations to local "Joe for Parliament" events.
- Team captains that meet their team door-to-door goal will receive two VIP tickets to our primary night party.

These responsibilities and benefits are just examples; we could make them whatever would be most beneficial to the campaign. The key with developing an organisation like this is giving people titles and real responsibilities, training them, providing them with materials, and then holding them accountable. Be sure that whatever you ask people to do, you give them all the training, support, and help you can to make sure they feel comfortable doing it. Nothing is worse than asking people to go door to door without telling them that you'll have a training session to show them how to do it.

## CANDIDATE TOURS

The campaign should plan a number of candidate tours to get Joe in front of as many voters as possible. Because CCS is a big constituency, the campaign should safeguard Joe's time by setting up multipurpose tours in various places that combine fundraising, media exposure, and vote-getting.

For example, if Joe is visiting Brofoyedur, the campaign could try to set up meetings with local NPP leaders, a press-invited tour of a local factory, a meal with a business leader/fundraising prospect, and some door to door campaign time.

## MEETING INFLUENTIAL PEOPLE

The campaign should develop a list of key influential throughout and target these leaders for meetings with Joe.

## ENDORSEMENTS

Because Joe is relatively unknown and new to politics in Cape Coast, key endorsements will be very helpful in establishing credibility. The campaign should use the meetings with influentials mentioned above to seek out endorsements that can then be publicised through earned and paid media.

## COALITION DEVELOPMENT

The campaign should seek to build coalitions that can help us spread our message and turn out voters. These coalitions can be based on age, issue, geography, or any other identifier but should always be consistent with our message. For example, if we're getting lots of support from senior citizens, we should start a "Seniors for Joe" coalition and appoint an active, supportive senior to chair the committee, which would hold events and perform volunteer work, etc. (These coalitions would fit in as part of the Joe's Team Captain program as a demographic team.)

## DOOR-TO-DOOR CAMPAIGNING

While the majority of Joe's time will not be spent going door to door, we always recommend that a candidate set aside thirty minutes per candidate tour day to go door to door—it's a great way to generate some buzz and keep the candidate connected with the voters.

While Joe will not be going door to door extensively, campaigning door to door will constitute a major part of our grassroots activities. All grassroots volunteers and team captains should be encouraged and trained to put together groups to go door to door on behalf of the campaign. The key to door-to-door campaigning is to make contact with as many voters as possible, as many times as possible.

Prior to beginning a door-to-door effort, the campaign should identify which doors to knock on. Focus on visiting voters in your targeted districts who have voted in at least two of the previous elections. This will prevent us from wasting the campaign's time and energy on non-voters. The campaign should also receive the voter list as a "walk list" organized by streets, with each side of the street listed separately.

*Note: Door-to-door campaigning should be done when people are home and available.*

The methodology for going door to door for your volunteers should be as follows:

1. Prepare materials for that day's canvassing.
2. Go door to door.
3. If a voter is home, present them with material and mark on your walk list that you talked with them. If they said they will support you, mark that down as well. Take notes. (*N.B.: Don't get bogged down talking to a voter for more than three or four minutes. If they want to talk longer, give them your phone number, invite them to call, and tell them you have to move on.)
4. After the day's canvassing is done, go back to HQ and enter the supporters you have marked down on to your supporter/get-out-the-vote list. Find opportunities to thank them.

The key for great door-to-door campaigning is to be well prepared, take great notes, and follow up immediately.

## VOTER BLITZES

Close to general election day, the campaign should use "voter blitzes" to raise name ID and campaign awareness. These voter blitzes are street events that require the help of at least ten to fifteen volunteers to accomplish successfully. These blitzes involve "invading" a neighbourhood or main street area where people congregate and pass by (preferably walk by). The volunteers should wave signs and hand out literature, and the local team captain should be there to shake hands and meet voters.

Voter blitzes should be fun, and often you can pass out sweets or some other treat. These blitzes should be scheduled for at least one hour during high-traffic times. The campaign should integrate these blitzes with door-to-door campaigning to maximise volunteer usage, by asking volunteers to come for the one-hour blitz, then going out for door-to-door campaigning for one to two hours.

## ELECTION-DAY/GET-OUT-THE-VOTE ACTIVITIES

One of the most important grassroots activities the campaign will operate will be our election-day/get-out-the-vote operation. It is imperative that we build up our grassroots organisation (Team Captain Program) so that these volunteers will be ready to work with us on election day.

As noted above, one of the key grassroots activities of the campaign will be developing a database of all of those people who we come in contact with who say they support us. This list should be growing constantly—every time Joe meets with someone, every time volunteers go door to door, every time someone makes a small contribution, those who donate or who explicitly say they support us should be noted in our campaign database. Once people are in the database, we should communicate with them to keep them interested and feeling like part of our "team". This keeps them involved and builds our relationship with them. Over the course of the campaign, they can be asked to volunteer, to donate, and to raise money on our behalf.

Our get-out-the-vote activities will also rely on this database of supporters. Our goal will be to contact these supporters in the days leading up to election day to make sure that they remember that it is election day and that they should go vote. Our goal is to make sure that as many of our supporters as possible go to the polls or mail in a ballot.

Our election-day/GOTV activities will include:

1. *Get-out-the-vote campaign.* The campaign should have a team of volunteers whose responsibility it is to contact each person that the campaign has identified as "supporters" to make sure they go vote. This will be accomplished through three methods.
    a. The weekend prior to election day, volunteers should call each person identified as a supporter to remind them that the election is on Tuesday and that they should go vote.
    b. The day before election day, the campaign should remind them.
    c. On election day, volunteers should spend the day going through the list again, and again call each supporter to remind them to go vote.

*Immediate action steps:*
- Start supporter file (database) for GOTV activities.
- Start calling contacts to find "super volunteers".
- Acquire necessary voter list.

## CAMPAIGN BUDGET

While this number is fluid and subject to change as the campaign progresses, the campaign should operate under the following preliminary campaign budget:

| Administration | ($) |
|---|---|
| Campaign database | 20,000 |
| Computer support | 20,000 |
| Rents | 175,000 |
| Utilities and phones | 100,000 |
| Travel | 125,000 |
| Equipment | 85,000 |
| Automobile | 20,000 |
| Furniture | 25,000 |
| Consultants | 150,000 |
| Staff | 1,250,000 |
| Polling | 100,000 |
| | |
| **Communications ($)** | |
| Website | 40,000 |
| Billboards | 125,000 |
| Radio | 400,000 |
| Television | 4,500,000 |
| Other printing and postage | 200,000 |
| | |
| **Fundraising** | ($) |
| Direct mail | 400,000 |
| Events | 250,000 |

| Volunteer program | 150,000 |
| Grassroots program | 200,000 |

For the purposes of campaign planning, it would be wise to use the above budget as our target budget, while employing an 80/20 budget rule—that is, we need to raise at least 80 per cent of the afformentioned budget ($7,668,000) to be competitive state-wide and raising 20 per cent more than our target budget ($11,502,000) would be our "dream" budget. For the minimum competitive budget, most cuts would come from the staff and communications lines. For our dream budget, most excess revenue would go towards communications tactics.

## FUNDRAISING PLAN

"Fundraising" isn't a dirty word. We've got a message and mission, one that is good for CCS. We've got a plan, and we know exactly how much it will cost to implement that plan. We need to raise the money to be competitive in this election. Now we need to go raise the money, and we needn't be bashful about doing it.

## GENERAL FUNDRAISING GUIDELINES

To meet our budget, we're going to have to work hard. Fundraising is hard work, but we've set a doable goal. Some general guidelines to keep in mind as we plan this effort:

- *You've gotta ask.* Very few people will offer contributions without ever being asked. The only way to raise money is to ask.

- *The candidate is fundraiser-in-chief.* Most people who give money will need to be asked by the candidate to do so. The easiest way for us to raise money is for the candidate to do the asking.
- *But he can't do it alone.* Joe can't do it all, though. He will need help. Cue the Finance Committee.
- *Ask for more than you think you will get.* Always ask a prospect for more money than you think they will give. Very few people will work their way up and give more than you ask for, but if you ask for too much and your prospect doesn't want to give that much, they can always work their way down and give less than you ask for.
- *Be concrete! Never ask for "a contribution".* Ask for $500. Never ask a prospect to "send the money when you get a chance." Ask, "Can I pick it from you today?" Be concrete in your requests and urgent in your appeals. That is the proven way to raise more money more effectively.
- *Go back for another bite.* If someone gives money to your campaign once, they are likely to do so again. We need to make sure we go back to our early donors to ask for money again later in the campaign.
- *Thank everyone.* Everyone who contributes should receive a thank-you note as soon as possible after the campaign receives their check.
- *Above all, do it!* Don't be shy. If our campaign doesn't raise the money it needs, Cape Coast South won't get what it really needs: independent leadership and real solutions.

The absolute best way for the campaign to raise money is for the candidate to ask for it personally, preferably over the phone or in person. We should begin fundraising through personal solicitation immediately. Joe should sit down with his contact list and mark off each person who he can call to give money to the campaign (should be 99 per cent of the people on your personal and business contact lists). Next to each name, write down how much you think each person can afford to give (not how much they will give). Then, add 20 per cent. This is our target number, the amount we will ask each person to give.

Joe should then spend a significant amount of time making calls. When someone answers, let them know you are running for office, tell them a bit about the campaign (spending one to two minutes on this), and let them know that it's going to cost us around $10000 to run a campaign that can win. Then make your ask. "Would you be willing to donate $500 to help us win this election?" (or whatever this specific ask is).

If the person says yes, ask them to send it immediately, or ask if you can pick it up. If the person says no, ask them if they can give a lesser amount. If they say no to that, ask them if they will help by volunteering their time. Whether they say yes or no, thank them, make a note of their answer, and move on.

At the end of your call session, send out a thank-you letter to each person who said yes. This thank-you letter should remind them of the amount of their pledge, and ask them to send it immediately.

Early in the campaign, the candidate should be spending 75 per cent of his time fundraising!

Not every call needs to be an ask. There are many, many people whom the campaign will want to meet in order to raise money from them at a later date. As explained as part of our on-site training, for these people, set up a "non-ask call" and then follow up with those people after you have established a relationship with them. The candidate should have a constant stream of people to call, either to ask for money, to introduce himself, or to follow up on a non-ask call.

## MAJOR DONOR GROUPS: THE FINANCE COMMITTEE

Developing a Finance Committee to help with our fundraising efforts will be extremely important in meeting our campaign goals. As Joe is combing through his personal contact list for his personal fundraising asks, he should also be thinking, *Who on this list can raise me money for the campaign?* This is our target list for the Finance Committee. Our goal should be to eventually find a finance chairman to head up the Finance Committee, someone who is asked to give/raise a significant amount for the campaign, and many, many Finance Committee members, who are asked to give/raise a minimum amount for the campaign.

When talking with Finance Committee prospects, let them know that you want them to be key members of your team, and that you will need their input on all aspects of the campaign, not just fundraising. Hold Finance Committee meetings once per month, at minimum, to motivate the committee and update them on the campaign.

Finance Committee members should be encouraged to make personal asks to their friends/contacts, hold fundraising events, and find other members to join our Finance Committee.

In addition to the Finance Committee, the campaign should seek opportunities to start other major donor groups that are industry, location, and demographic specific.

## EVENTS

Events provide a key way of reaching mid- and small-level donors in a relatively easy fashion. Finance Committee members and other supporters should be encouraged to host in-home fundraising events on behalf of the campaign. Be sure to make it clear to these event hosts that we expect them to invite their own friends and contacts to the event.

Many supporters will want to host fundraising events but then expect the campaign to invite its own prospects. This isn't helpful. We need to expand our fundraising universe, and the best way to do that is to get your supporters to invite their contacts to a small fundraising event on our behalf.

Events can range from ten people at $25 per person to a five-person sit-down dinner at $1,000 per person and everything in between. The key is to schedule as many of these events as possible as early in the campaign cycle as possible.

No matter who hosts the event, the campaign should get contact information for everyone who comes, include all donors on our supporter list for get-out-the-vote efforts, and send thank-you notes to everyone who contributed.

## INTERNET FUNDRAISING

The campaign should actively promote the donation option to visitors to the campaign website. Also consider using e-mail fundraising solicitations sent to our e-mail supporter list.

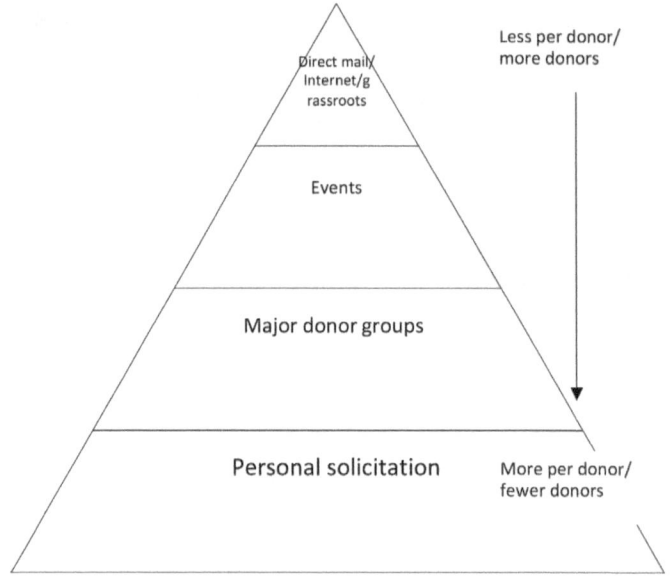

## REVENUE GOALS

The campaign's revenue goals for each fundraising method should be as follows:

Personal solicitation: $4,250,000
Major donor groups: $2,500,000
Events: $1,500,000
Internet fundraising: $250,000
Total: $8,500,000

*As can clearly be seen from these goals, Joe's calls and meetings will form a major portion of our fundraising revenue.
  *Immediate action steps:*
  • Put together personal solicitation prospect list.

- Put together finance chairman and Finance Committee prospect list.
- Start making calls!

## IDEAL CAMPAIGN TIMELINES

Staffing/consultants
1. Candidate (done)
2. Campaign manager (done)
3. Campaign treasurer and legal counsel (immediately)
4. General consultant (immediately)
5. Finance director (September 2015)
6. Direct mail, media, and polling consultants sign-up (September 2015)
7. Communications director (October 2014)
8. Volunteer director (November 2014)
9. Field director (January 2015)
10. Director of campaign research (February 2013)
11. Director of administration (February 2014)

## FUNDRAISING TIMELINES

Ideal fundraising goals: Estimated amounts required to run ideal campaign strategy according to this plan (total amount raised by campaign/target date).

$100,000/1 October 2013
$500,000/15 December 2014
$8,000,000/1 October 2014

With your plan in place, success is as good as how you implement the plan.

## CONCLUSION

This manual provides a great deal of information. Even if you read through the manual first and then work through it step by step, taking the time to write a campaign plan, you will probably still miss some important points. It is impossible to foresee all that will happen in the campaign, even if you have past political experience. You should refer back to this manual, just as you should refer back to your campaign plan, as the campaign progresses and questions arise.

A political campaign should not be a mere series of events and activities haphazardly sequenced and arbitrarily timed. It should be rolled out with clear purpose as part of a logical plan.

Over the years, political campaigns have become increasingly professional, specialised and complex operations. You should not attempt to launch a campaign without a clear written plan any more than you would launch construction of an office without architectural and engineering plans.

Approaching the complications of most campaigns is a daunting task for candidates, managers, and staff. To do it, you have to break the whole operation down into separate, understandable, manageable components. As the old saying goes, you eat an elephant, no matter how large, one piece at a time.

Let me reiterate that campaign plans are great tools and just that; they do not replace the everyday tasks of talking to voters and selling the candidate. No campaign, no matter how small, should be without one. They provide guidance, timelines, and budgets and generally should be followed in the successful pursuit of elected office.

Writing a comprehensive plan is not only a starting point to ensuring victory on election day, but it also imposes a sense of order on a process that can otherwise be chaotic and confusing.

It can be done. If you fail to plan, you plan to fail. Remember, there is no "prize" for runners-up in political campaigning. If you lose, the whole team loses.

# ABOUT THE AUTHOR'S

## KOJO YANKAH

Kojo Yankah is a motivational speaker, speechwriter, debate coach, pollster and campaign strategist. He has a broad range of experience in political campaign strategy, communications planning, grassroots tactics, and fundraising.

His accomplishments include working as a consultant for several major political campaigns. Over the past decade, he has consulted with dozens of political campaigns to help them win.

Kojo has strategically advised several prestigious campaigns, including NPP UK Chairman Michael Ansah, Western Regional Secretary of NPP Charles Bissiue, First Vice Chairman of NPP UK Jojo Blankson, MP for Yagba-Kubori, Mustapha Ussif, and Shirley Kyei, NPP UK Women Organiser, among others.

Though his consulting work has focused on New Patriotic Party candidates, this book is non-partisan. It teaches political strategy and tactics that work for all candidates, regardless of political affiliation.

Authoring several articles on political campaign strategy, Kojo has advised and directed scores of candidates and campaign managers on how to successfully win an election.

Raised in Ghana, Kojo earned a BA Hons from University of Ghana, an MSc from Queen Mary University of London, and a PGCE Post-Compulsory from Canterbury Christ Church University, London.

## DODZIE NUMEKEVOR

**Dodzie Numekevor is a Communications specialist, Political campaign strategist and a grassroots political mobilisation expert.**

**He was constituency secretary of the ruling New Patriotic Party and the campaign strategist for the constituency's winning campaign in the 2000 elections. Dodzie served on the national campaign team as a personal assistant to the late Jake Obetsebi Lamptey, then national campaign manager.**

**He was also a campaign advisor for the Michael Ansah bid for the NPP UK chairmanship. Dodzie is also a partner at AFRICONOMIE, a frontier markets investment advisory firm based in London.**

**Dodzie was born in Ghana, gained a Diploma in Communications from the Ghana Institute of Journalism, LLB(Hons) with International Development from the London Metropolitan University and a BPTC candidate with the Honorable Society of the Middle Temple.**